ARMY
BE THE BEST
REGULAR & TERRITORIAL

BE THE BEST
...at just about everything

The **ULTIMATE** Army guide to surviving modern life

Published by Century 2008

2 4 6 8 10 9 7 5 3 1

First published in Great Britain in 2008 by: Century, Random House, 20 Vauxhall Bridge Road, London SW1V 2SA

www.randomhouse.co.uk

Addresses for companies within The Random House Group Limited can be found at: www.randomhouse.co.uk

The Random House Group Limited Reg. No. 954009

A CIP catalogue record for this book is available from the British Library

ISBN 9781846055553

The Random House Group Limited supports The Forest Stewardship Council (FSC), the leading international forest certification organisation. All our titles that are printed on Greenpeace approved FSC certified paper carry the FSC logo. Our paper procurement policy can be found at: www.rbooks.co.uk/environment

Printed and bound in Italy by L.E.G.O. S.p.A

ARMY

BE THE BEST
...at just about everything

About this book

The British Army is respected the world over. That's no surprise when you consider the amazing range of experience and expertise it has.

As well as the things you'd expect it to know a thing or two about – surviving outdoors, jumping out of planes, keeping fit – the Army boasts hundreds of different skills that aren't as immediately obvious.

It has its own doctors and dentists, electricians and engineers. It has carpenters and chefs, signallers and scientists. There are drivers and divers, musicians and physicians – the list goes on.

That's before we've even talked about courage, leadership, initiative – values British soldiers are renowned for. All in all, there's not a skill out there that the Army doesn't have covered.

This book gives you access to this world of knowledge. There are hundreds of pieces of priceless advice contained in these pages – and every one is backed up by the British Army.

Whether you're a practical type looking to build a shed (tip 16), an outdoor sort hot on smoke signalling (tip 78), or if you're just happy to greet your friends in Swahili (tip 260), you're guaranteed to find inspiration inside.

With this book in your pocket, you're equipped for whatever challenges – indoors or outdoors, everyday or unusual, physical or mental – modern life has to throw at you.

And you'll have the British Army right behind you.

01

Cross a crocodile-infested swamp

Crocs are fast and bad tempered. Don't make any snap decisions to swim with them!

1 Stand back
Don't stray too near the water's edge to plot your route across the river. Crocs rely on surprise to catch their prey, resembling driftwood as they glide towards the shore. One flick of the tail is enough to knock a human into the water.

2 Run for it
Crocodiles can reach speeds of up to 7mph over short distances on land. If a crocodile runs at you, your best bet is to sprint away from it in a straight line. Don't zigzag to try to shake it off, and make sure you run away from water.

3 Time to fight
Crocs can hold their breath for a long time so tend to drag their prey underwater and spin them round to kill them. If you end up on the receiving end of a death roll go for the eyes – the most sensitive part of a crocodile – or the nostrils and ears.

02
Cook a worm omelette

Why worms?
Earthworms are a good protein source, and much easier to 'catch' than wild game like rabbits. But they're low on calories, so should only form part of a survival diet.

Find and prepare
Rich soil will contain hundreds of earthworms per square metre: dig down until the earth becomes damp then start sifting with your fingers. When you've got a handful, toss them into boiling water – this will quickly kill, clean and cook them. After one minute, drain the water.

Cook it all up
Lightly whisk three eggs with a fork, adding plenty of salt and pepper – worms taste a little bland. Heat a frying pan and warm some butter or oil. Add the eggs and, as the mixture sets, toss in the worms. Fold the omelette over and cook on both sides until golden. Enjoy!

Step 1

Step 2

Step 3

03
Drink from a cactus

1 Prickly pears

Prickly pears — made up of flat, rounded pads — are common in the Americas. Harvest the youngest, greenest pads, peel off their skins (wear gloves!) and eat raw. The soft flesh is watery, nutritious and tastes like green peppers.

2 Columnar cacti

Columnar cacti (which grow in tall columns), such as the Saguaro, contain moist flesh under tough exteriors. Simply lop off a limb, trim the edges and suck out the juice. (Saguaro cacti are a protected species, so only try this in a real emergency!)

3 Barrel cacti

Slice the top off a short, fat 'barrel' cactus and scoop or cut out the flesh. Mash the flesh up and force it through a cloth and you should be able to filter out a gluey liquid that tastes something like raw vegetables. Mmm, cactus smoothie.

04
Disguise your own smell

1 Neutralise your niffs
Wash your hair (tip 42), armpits and feet to get rid of any natural body odours – but only use scent-free soap and shampoo. Don't dry off with a fabric-softened towel, don't use toothpaste (baking soda is an odour-free alternative) and don't chew gum.

2 Deodorise your clothes
Wash your clothes in water only (tip 100), and air them naturally (don't tumble-dry).

3 Adapt to the environment
In the field, smear your skin and clothing with locally occurring mud or foliage.

05
Shoe a horse

- Remove the old shoe using a pair of 'pull offs' (pliers) and trim the hoof, just like you'd cut your fingernails.
- Choose a correctly sized replacement shoe and fine-tune the fit by bending it. The 'hot shoe' method – heating it in the forge – is the most accurate.
- Hammer the shoe on cold, slanting the nails outward so they exit the hoof before penetrating its sensitive inner tissue.
- Snip off any exposed nails, then use a rasp to file down the shoe so that no metal overlaps the shape of the hoof. Job done, you're back in the saddle.

BE THE BEST...

06
Parachute from a plane

■ Go to the loo before you board. Your jumpsuit can't be easily taken off and staring down from an open doorway at 2500 feet can speed up anyone's bowel movements.

■ Pay attention to your jump master, your commander on the plane. Follow their orders.

■ Orientate yourself as the plane climbs. Make sure you know where you're supposed to land. Pick out a landmark that will help you find it. The situation can change without warning.

■ Your jump master will take your static line (which will open your parachute safely) and clip it to a wire in the aircraft. Check that it is securely clipped.

■ When the pilot feathers the engine, it's your turn. In the Army it's a military offence to refuse to jump – but you can still say no at this point.

■ Get into the correct exit position (you'll have rehearsed this on the ground simulator). Exit robustly (give it a good leap!) and remember the golden rule: keep your legs and feet tightly together. This will prevent serious twists of your rigging lines. Count six seconds by shouting "one thousand, two thousand, three thousand..." Your chute should open automatically after six seconds. Look up to check the canopy is fully open. Look all around to make sure you are in clear airspace and not drifting towards anyone else.

■ Now enjoy one of the most amazing sensations there is.

07
Make a ball from a goat's bladder

■ Butcher a goat. Extract the bladder, leaving an inch or so of the urethra (the tube that extends from the bladder) intact. Wash inside and out.

■ Without letting the bladder dry out, blow it up like a balloon (use a straw if you're squeamish). It will stretch a remarkable amount.

■ Once the bladder is taut and roughly conforming to FA regulations, swiftly tie it off at the urethra. Game on!

08
Lie still for eight hours

Army reconnaissance experts need to hole up unobserved for days at a time. Here's how they do it:

1 Choose your spot

If possible, pick your location in advance and move into it at daybreak. You'll need to be able to take in the whole field of view without moving anything other than your head. Remove any stones – even the smallest pebble under your body can cause excruciating pain after a couple of hours – and line your 'nest' with soft grass, leaves and moss. And don't forget to empty bladder and bowels before getting into position!

2 Get camouflaged

Use foliage to disguise your outline (tip 203) and protect your head from the elements. Carry nothing shiny or straight – both will scream 'man-made!' in a natural environment. Make sure all your gear is easily to hand, as any sort of movement greatly increases the chance of detection.

3 Settle in

Keep your blood moving by flexing fingers and toes, and rock your body as slowly as possible over the day. Keep your mind alert by scanning the ground, but don't lose focus and drift off into mind games.

09
Use the sun as a compass

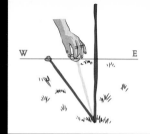

1 The shadow stick

Hammer a tall stick into flat ground. Mark the top of its shadow with a stone. Wait 30 minutes, see where the shadow has moved to and mark the top of it with a second stone. A line between the two stones runs approximately west to east (east to west in the southern hemisphere).

2 The super shadow stick

A more accurate version. Set up your stick as before and place a stone at the end of the shadow some time in the morning. Using a length of thread tied to the base of the stick, draw a large arc that sweeps through the point where the stone is. As the sun moves east to west the shadow will move the opposite way, shortening until noon and then starting to lengthen. At the point in the afternooon when the tip of the stick's shadow reaches the arc once more, mark it with a second stone. The line between the stones runs west to east.

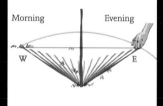

3 The magic watch

If you're in the northern hemisphere, point the hour hand of your watch at the sun. Imagine another hand pointing to the '12' (in the UK, during British Summer Time imagine a hand pointing to the '1'). The line directly between the two hands will be pointing due south, with north directly opposite. Clever, eh?

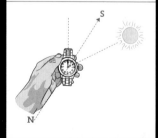

10
Get a six-pack

Everybody has abs – honestly, they're under there somewhere. Exercising will help you burn the fat off, and a sensible low-fat diet is crucial in the long term.

Then it's all down to setting out a regular abdominal workout programme and sticking to it. Mix up the following three exercises for 20-30 minutes, three or four times a week:

1 Sit-ups
Tip 56 shows you how to do a PTI-perfect sit-up. As with all these exercises, you'll need to increase the number you do in a session as you get stronger. Once you've built up enough strength to make normal sit-ups easy, try doing them while holding a small weight on your chest – you can build up to heavier weights.

2 Crunches
Lie down with arms crossed on your chest. Draw in your abdomen while breathing in, then lift your shoulders off the floor using only the abdominal muscles. Breathe out as your shoulders rise and hold them off the floor for a moment, but don't try to sit up fully. Then gently lower your shoulders back to the floor. Repeat.

3 Leg lifts
This time sit up, resting on your elbows at your sides. Lift your legs up to an angle of 45° without bending the knees, then lower them slowly without letting them touch the floor. Repeat. A good variant is to put your hands by your head, elbows pointing at your feet, and 'cycle' with your legs, so the knees touch the elbows.

Apache helicopter
pilot helmet

11
Wear a hat

From berets to bearskins, parading to
patrolling, soldiers know how to wear
a hat. So should you.

Wearing a hat is all about feeling
comfortable. If you feel good, you'll exude
confidence. If you feel ridiculous, you risk
looking that way. So it's essential to choose
a hat you like. Get a second opinion from
someone you trust, and then back yourself.

There are other factors that can assist
you in carrying off the behatted look. What
kind of face have you got? (Be honest with
yourself!) If you have a small face, avoid
big hats and large brims. A small, tight hat
will accentuate the features of a large face.

Know your head measurement and buy a
hat of the right size. The angle you wear it at
can make you look jaunty or serious. And
choose the right hat for the occasion – a
sombrero is fun at a festival, not at a funeral.

Comfortable = confident = cool.

Officer 'Passing Out' hat

Turban

Bearskin (foot guards)

Caubeen (Irish regiments)

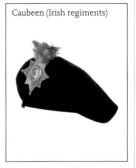

Household Cavalry helmet

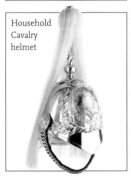

Glengarry (Royal Regiment of Scotland)

Ghurka hat

12
Be tidy

Being tidy is a frame of mind, not a physical attribute. A tidy mind leads to a tidy life, and the less clutter you have in your life, the easier it is to organise.

First things first, get rid of what you don't need. Old toys, clothes you never wear, half-read Sunday supplements from months ago, chuck 'em out.

Next, designate a specific place for different categories of your belongings. If you have hundreds of DVDs, keep them all on the same shelves. Same with books, CDs, gadgets, paperwork, you name it – keep your personal belongings like a chef keeps his kitchen: in order.

Junk piles up. Bundle of dirty clothes by your bed? Get it in the wash basket ASAP. Unopened letters piling up on the kitchen table? Take five minutes out of your busy Xbox 360 schedule to go through them and bin what you don't need.

Make sure your home has plenty of storage space and containers. If it doesn't, find space and buy the containers. If you still can't keep it tidy, you officially have too much stuff.

13
Vault a wall

Running from a bull or tackling an obstacle course, sometimes you'll want to vault a wall or gate at speed. Here's how it's done:

1 Don't run straight at the wall, slow your pace a touch and run parallel to it. Put your nearest hand on the wall.

2 Look where you want to land.

3 Use your momentum to throw your legs up. You should lead with the leg nearest to the wall, then the other. Don't lean back. Use the hand you placed on the wall to guide your body.

4 If you've done it right, you should land over the wall.

5 Keep on running!

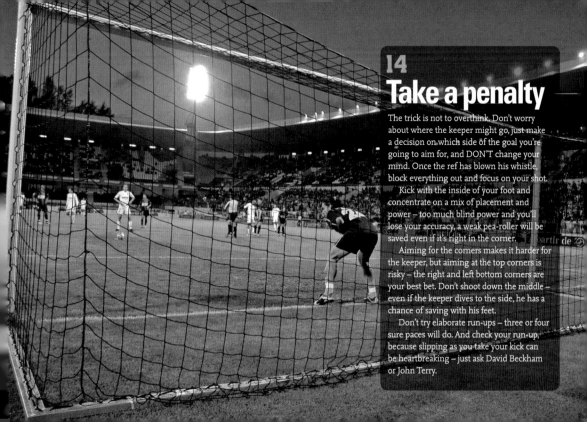

14
Take a penalty

The trick is not to overthink. Don't worry about where the keeper might go, just make a decision on which side of the goal you're going to aim for, and DON'T change your mind. Once the ref has blown his whistle, block everything out and focus on your shot.

Kick with the inside of your foot and concentrate on a mix of placement and power – too much blind power and you'll lose your accuracy, a weak pea-roller will be saved even if it's right in the corner.

Aiming for the corners makes it harder for the keeper, but aiming at the top corners is risky – the right and left bottom corners are your best bet. Don't shoot down the middle – even if the keeper dives to the side, he has a chance of saving with his feet.

Don't try elaborate run-ups – three or four sure paces will do. And check your run-up, because slipping as you take your kick can be heartbreaking – just ask David Beckham or John Terry.

15
Climb a rope

1 Grab the rope with both hands above your head.
2 Pull down on the rope and jump to hoist yourself into the air.
3 Wrap the rope around one leg and use your feet to grip the rope, anchoring yourself.
4 Reach up high and grip the rope tightly, one hand at a time.
5 Release the rope from your feet. Using your abdominals, bring your knees up to your chest. Re-secure your feet on the rope.

6 Stand up with your legs, gripping tightly with your feet, reaching as high as possible with your arms.
7 Repeat the process until the top of the rope has been reached.
8 To come down, loosen the grip of your feet on the rope. Support weight evenly between your feet and hands, slide your feet down and place hand over hand on the way down.

16
Build a shed

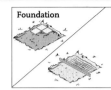
Foundation

Floor

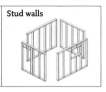
Stud walls

- A good foundation is fundamental. Lay concrete or alternatively use a layer of paving slabs. Your foundation must be level and keep the wood of your shed off the ground and away from water.

- At the timber yard choose: softwood for the floor joists and stud walls, plywood for the floor (use exterior plywood with a minimum thickness of 15mm) and shiplap to cover the walls (this is a version of tongue and groove planking where each plank fits under the overlapping edge of the plank above it, a design that keeps water out better). Coat all timber in preservative.

- Construct four stud walls with 2in x 4in timber (a stud wall is the wooden framework of the wall to which you will later secure your shiplap planking). It's best not to spread your uprights too far apart otherwise the shiplap will bend. Brace the uprights with cross members called noggins to make the stud wall stronger.

- Make your floor in a similar way to the stud walls and cover with plywood. Attach your four walls to the base and secure. If you are on your own it is easier to nail the walls but screws are much stronger.

- Nail the shiplap timber onto the walls using small nails. Line your walls with waterproof paper to keep the interior extra dry.

- Add the roof. A pitched roof like that of a house will give you more headroom in the middle.

- Have a quiet cuppa inside.

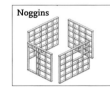
Noggins

Build

Roof

Exterior

Cuppa!

17
Survive a week in the forest

For whatever reason you are sleeping in the open, be prepared. By having at the very least a tent or shelter, a good knife, matches and a compass you should emerge from your week in the forest intact.

Your priorities are water, food, fire, shelter and rescue.

Water
Find it, ascertain whether it's drinkable, and if not then make it so (tip 197).

Food
Eat insects less than an inch in length raw, but larger ones should be cooked (tip 265). Remove parts that might hook you on the way down. Don't eat mushrooms or yellow and white berries. If you're not sure whether to eat something, rub it on your skin and look for any adverse reaction first before trying it in the corner of your mouth, on the tip of your tongue and finally by eating a small piece.

Fire
Get a good fire going for warmth, for cooking and for boiling water. Make sure you have the means and skills to make a fire (tip 51).

Shelter
If you don't have a tent you can cut branches for a windbreak or make a shelter (tip 206). Natural resources for shelter include hollows, stones, fallen boughs and saplings lashed together. Snow can be packed into an insulating shelter too. Have a point zero (safe, near water) you can always find your way back to.

Rescue
If help is on the way, stay in one place. You might need to signal to potential rescuers.

18

Put a crease in your trousers

Assuming you don't have a trouser press, your next best ally for this is a brown paper bag. Plus, of course, a good iron and ironing board.

A crease should run from your front belt loop down to the hem. Lightly wet the trouser leg along your intended crease, then lay the paper bag over the top and press down hard with the iron on a hot setting, moving carefully along from hem to belt loop. The crease should last months.

19
Save money

You can't switch on a TV, surf the net or walk down the street without being bombarded with adverts imploring you to buy things. So how do you keep your wants from your needs, and tighten those purse strings?

Set your target

What are you saving for? A ski trip? A PS3? A festival ticket? Before you start to stash the cash, work out your goals and when you hope to achieve them. That way you can structure your saving habits and keep track.

Keep records

Calculate your monthly income and outgoings. List all your regular bills and payments. Try to clear outstanding debts, starting with those charging highest interest. Keep track of your bank statements and you'll know how close you are to your goals. Budget for everything.

Live sensibly

Cutting down on just a small amount of the good life can save you plenty in the long run (and it's not bad for your health either). Work out where you can trim the fat. Cut down on unnecessary expenses and keep track of your priorities.

Don't forego life's pleasures – you can treat yourself once in a while – but remember the ultimate goal whenever you feel yourself dipping into the funds. All the pain will be worth it when you can buy what you're after.

A	Alpha	N	November
B	Bravo	O	Oscar
C	Charlie	P	Papa
D	Delta	Q	Quebec
E	Echo	R	Romeo
F	Foxtrot	S	Sierra
G	Golf	T	Tango
H	Hotel	U	Uniform
I	India	V	Victor
J	Juliet	W	Whisky
K	Kilo	X	X-ray
L	Lima	Y	Yankee
M	Mike	Z	Zulu

20
Understand phonetics

Used by the military, police, pilots and other communicators so there is no confusion over letters, the standard NATO phonetic alphabet was adopted by civil aviation as long ago as 1956. To enable it to be understood internationally, each word has sounds that are common to English, French and Spanish.

21
Help at a road traffic accident

One moment you're standing at the traffic lights waiting to cross the road, the next you're faced with a car accident and injured pedestrians. Snap out of your shock and do the following:

1 Make the area safe. Set up traffic control and a cordon to keep pedestrians and vehicles away if necessary.

2 Call emergency services. Report exactly what you see, and they'll know what to send.

3 Recruit fellow bystanders to assist.

4 Give first aid to the casualties, prioritising the most seriously injured. Be careful not to move anyone, unless their life is clearly at risk from their surroundings. But you can at least try to make them comfortable until paramedics arrive.

5 Make a note of events. You may be called upon as a witness when the dust settles.

22
Ski

1 Start on a small slope, pointing your ski tips close together and the ski tails wide apart to form a wedge, or 'snow plough'. This will keep your speed down. Later, when you want to pick up speed, you can position your skis parallel to each other. If you start going too fast, switch back to the snow plough.

2 Turning. Take a little weight off the leg in the direction you want to turn. So to turn right, lift your right heel a little. Never cross your skis – this is the fastest way to take a tumble.

3 Keep your knees slightly bent to control your weight. Look ahead, not at your feet. If you're about to crash into something and you're a beginner, don't swerve – you'll probably hit something else. Fall over instead.

4 Those are the basics. Practice your skills as much as possible.

23
Be a leader

Leaders don't fit one mould, but they often have certain qualities in common.

1 Lead from the front

The best lead by example, not by shouting orders. You'll earn the respect of others by rolling up your sleeves and getting your hands dirty. You should always be a role model.

2 Build a strong team around you

Skilful leaders draw talented people around them and listen to them. There's nothing weak in making the most of others' talents. You don't have to have all the good ideas but you do need to recognise a good idea when you see it, and not be too proud to use it.

3 Don't be afraid to praise or criticise

Those around you need to know what they're doing right and wrong. Work with them to build on their strengths and improve their weaknesses. Try to look for the positive in people, however bad they might be – set them achievable goals to improve.

4 Act decisively

In times of crisis, others will look to you for direction. Think quickly but carefully, decide on the right course of action and pursue it with conviction.

24
Make small talk

Awkward silences are... awkward. Learn to keep the conversation flowing with anyone you meet.

1 Practise
Talk to everyone you come across: waiters, cashiers, neighbours, people in queues. Conversation is like anything else – the more you practise, the better you'll get.

2 Information is ammo
Read everything – newspapers, books, magazines, reviews, even catalogues. The more information you have, the more you can chat about.

3 Listen up
Become a better listener. People easily reveal clues about themselves. Learn to pick up on these hints and turn them into topics of conversation.

4 Avoid controversy
If you're talking to a stranger, stay away from negative or controversial topics. If they say something very offensive, it's probably a conversation to avoid.

5 Answer with questions
If you're asked a question, don't just give a short answer. Embellish it and make it interesting, and answer with a question if you can. This will draw the other person in and set up a conversational tennis match.

25
Do the perfect press-up

Method:

- Lie on your stomach. Place your hands on the floor just outside your shoulders, fingers spread and elbows pointing up. Your toes need to be flexed and feet slightly apart.
- Taking your body weight on your arms and shoulders, push yourself up from the ground until your arms are straight.
- Hold your position for a second. Then lower yourself back down until your elbows reach 90° and your chest is about two inches from the floor.
- Push back up to begin your next press-up.

Tips:

- Keep your body in a straight line throughout the movement (don't stick your backside in the air or arch your back).
- Inhale as you push up and exhale as you lower yourself. Don't hold your breath.
- Concentrate on good technique rather than speed – you'll get more benefit.
- Try to progressively increase the number of press-ups you can do in a row each time you exercise.

Muscle groups worked:
Shoulders, chest, upper arms, stomach

26
Shave in the field

If all you have to hand is a blade, shaving is not going to be a picnic. Water alone is not very good at softening stubble because it is repelled by the hair's natural oils, so even a speck of soap will be better than nothing.

Otherwise, try to soak your chin for as long as possible, then lean over a static pool of water and be prepared for a few cuts. A small bottle of oil, or even gun oil, will make for a more comfortable field shave.

Alternatively, take the opportunity to grow a manly beard.

27
Track a human

Of all the creatures on the planet, the human is often the easiest to track. Unless professionally trained, your average Joe Bloggs will leave plenty of clumsy signs, even if attempting to cover his tracks.

Try moving silently through a forest and you'll realise how difficult it is to keep perfectly quiet. This is where it pays to keep your ears open as well as your eyes. Listen for any movement and pay particular attention to any disturbances.

People usually watch where they're placing they're feet but not necessarily what they might be brushing against, so check for signs of disturbance above ankle height, right down to broken spiderwebs on your path.

Other animals want to keep a clear distance from humans so watch for any startled birds taking to the skies, and don't get too excited if you find clear footprints on the ground – it could be a decoy to lead you in the wrong direction.

28
Climb a six-foot wall

The six-foot wall is a standard feature of an Army obstacle course… and here's how to conquer it:

1 Run towards the wall at a steady jog.

2 Jump up and place both your forearms on top of the wall, gripping the far edge.

3 Hurl one leg up on top of the wall.

4 Pull yourself onto the top of the wall (soldiers are taught to keep low to the top of the wall to avoid potential enemy fire).

5 Swivel round so your legs are hanging over the far side and you are gripping the near edge of the wall with your fingers.

6 Turn around so you are looking where you will land. Push off and jump to the ground feet first, landing with knees bent.

29
Tie a slip knot

While not the strongest of knots, the slip knot (also known as a running knot) is very versatile. If you have nimble fingers it can even be tied with one hand, making it ideal for securing light items during climbing. Just don't place anything of great importance on the end of it – certainly not your own weight. It's called the slip knot because the knot can easily be pulled (slipped) out.

- Hold a length of rope in front of you and twist to form a loop.
- Fold the loop backwards to create two loops side by side.
- Put one loop through the other and pull tight.
- You now have a loop that can be placed around something and the knot can be tightened against it. Pulling the other way will loosen or untie it.

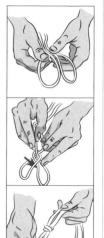

30

Clear a path through a jungle

You can't swing from tree to tree, so you're going to have to take this forest on foot.

You will need a machete. Only cut when you have to in order to conserve energy, and stroke upwards to do it as this reduces noise – you don't want everything in the jungle knowing where you are.

Move smoothly and steadily, turning your shoulders and shifting your hips to slide between the undergrowth.

Part vegetation with a stick or your machete rather than by hand – this way you won't get pricked by thorns and the stick will also dislodge anything that might bite you.

Take your bearings regularly – it's easy to lose your way.

When you stop, look through the forest to see if there are any paths open, and examine the jungle floor for game trails to follow.

31
Tie a strong knot

1 Take two pieces of rope. Make an open loop out of the end of the first piece, roughly three inches long. (If one piece is thicker than the other, make the loop out of this piece, because this takes most of the tension of the knot.)

2 Thread the end of the second piece of rope through the loop and then over the loop's short end.

3 Now bring the end of the second piece of rope underneath both sides of the open loop.

4 Next, bring the end of the second piece of rope round and over the long side of the loop, back under itself and then over the short side of the loop.

5 Pull on the two short ends to set the knot. Then pull all parts of the rope tight so the knot is nice and secure. You have tied a 'sheet bend' knot.

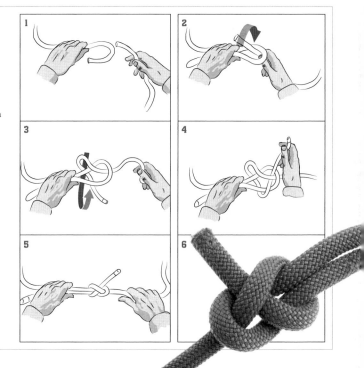

BE THE BEST...

"DON'T EVEN THINK ABOUT TRYING TO OUTRUN A TWISTER"

32
Survive a tornado

Tornadoes bring swirling winds of over 300mph, which can destroy solid brick walls. So the best way to survive one is not to be anywhere near it. That means avoiding the 'Tornado Alley' states of southern and central USA, especially during late spring.

If you are holed up in Kansas and a tornado watch has been announced, look out for unusual changes in the behaviour of cats and dogs, and for the sky becoming suddenly birdless. Then listen out for a deep rumbling noise… and make sure you know where the cellar door is.

No access to a cellar or basement? Stay in the least exposed room available (avoid buildings with large roofs), keep away from windows and doors, and hide under the heaviest piece of furniture you can find.

If you're in a car, don't even think about trying to outrun a twister. With luck, you'll have time to get to a substantial building. Otherwise, park up safely, jump into a narrow ditch and use your arms to protect your head from falling debris. There will be lots of it.

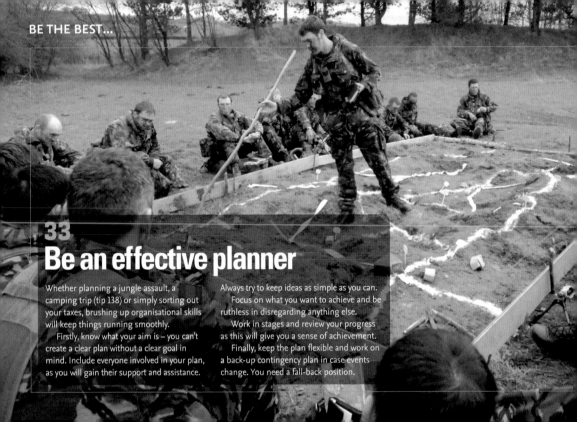

33
Be an effective planner

Whether planning a jungle assault, a camping trip (tip 138) or simply sorting out your taxes, brushing up organisational skills will keep things running smoothly.

Firstly, know what your aim is – you can't create a clear plan without a clear goal in mind. Include everyone involved in your plan, as you will gain their support and assistance.

Always try to keep ideas as simple as you can.

Focus on what you want to achieve and be ruthless in disregarding anything else.

Work in stages and review your progress as this will give you a sense of achievement.

Finally, keep the plan flexible and work on a back-up contingency plan in case events change. You need a fall-back position.

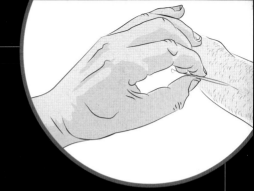

34
Remove a splinter

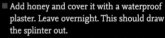

If the tip of the splinter is sticking out, grip it with clean fingernails or tweezers and carefully pull it out; don't break it.

When the splinter is buried under the skin, try one of these removal methods:

- Squeeze the surrounding area to work the splinter to the surface.
- Have a warm bath; this can open the pores and ease the splinter to the surface.
- Pour white glue over the splinter. When it's dry, peel it away and the splinter may come too.
- Apply Sellotape or duct tape to the area; this can pull out a splinter fast.

- Add honey and cover it with a waterproof plaster. Leave overnight. This should draw the splinter out.
- Left overnight, the sticky end of a fabric plaster can draw a splinter out.
- Apply plenty of magnesium sulphate paste (from a chemist) to the area, cover with a plaster and leave overnight. This draws the splinter to the surface. Or use baking soda and water in place of magnesium sulphate.
- If you can stand a bit of pain, reach for a sterilised needle. Try to get the tip of the needle under the end of the splinter to lever it out. You'll need to dig away skin. Note: never use an unsterilised needle.

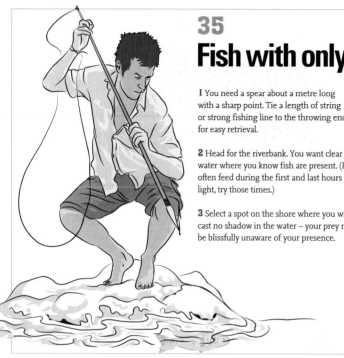

35
Fish with only a spear

1 You need a spear about a metre long with a sharp point. Tie a length of string or strong fishing line to the throwing end for easy retrieval.

2 Head for the riverbank. You want clear water where you know fish are present. (Fish often feed during the first and last hours of light, try those times.)

3 Select a spot on the shore where you will cast no shadow in the water – your prey must be blissfully unaware of your presence.

4 Look closely and wait (patience is needed) for a sizeable fish to appear and linger.

5 Compensating for the light bending in water – the fish will appear closer than it is to the surface – launch your spear hard at your target. Throw the spear from as close to the water as you can.

6 If you are successful you will spear through the fish. It will wriggle like crazy at first so get it ashore as smoothly and quickly as you can. Hit it on the back of the head with a stone or the blunt side of a knife to kill it quickly.

7 Time to gut it (tip 119).

36
Read a compass

A compass will always point to magnetic north (unless you're in the southern hemisphere, or happen to be standing next to a giant magnet). The 'pointing' end of the needle will usually be red. Lay the compass flat – on your map if you have one – and line up the needle with the pointer arrow. That's north. Rotate your map the same way and you'll be out of those woods in no time.

37
Stay awake all night

- Prepare in advance by pushing back your bedtime, night by night.
- Caffeine is your friend. Drink a cup of tea or coffee or have a can of cola 90 minutes before you'd normally hit the sack, and another 30 minutes before. Repeat as necessary.
- Occupy your mind. Set yourself tasks, play brain games – anything to keep mentally busy. Go for a walk. Phone a friend on the other side of the world. Watch a DVD (not a boring one!).
- Stimulate your body by turning down the temperature, keeping yourself hungry or seeing how long you can maintain a full bladder. Listen to loud music and keep the lights bright.
- If you feel yourself drifting off, stick a fingernail into your palm – nothing wakes you up like pain.
- Don't relax! Don't sit down or 'experiment' by closing your eyes. Next thing you know, it'll be morning…

38
Paddle your own kayak

Kayaking is a fun and exciting adventure sport. It takes a heck of a lot of training and practice, though, to get good enough to ride the raging rapids like the Army wildwater team member pictured.

So forget that and start with the basics. You'll need to learn from an instructor in the far more mundane but far safer environment of a swimming pool, with the added safety of a life jacket.

First you need to learn how to get in and out of the kayak without capsizing – stabilise the kayak by resting a paddle across it and the shore. Once you've mastered that and developed a sense of balance, learn how to paddle. The technique involves alternating strokes to the right and left of the boat, rolling the wrists between strokes so the blade enters the water correctly (the blades are set at different angles to one another on the paddle).

The first part of your stroke, from the moment the paddle dips into the water until it is level with your hips, provides forward power. Continuing the stroke back behind the hips makes you start to steer the kayak towards the side you are stroking on.

You will also be taught very early on how to perform a 'wet exit' – how to get out of your kayak if it capsizes (which it will).

Once you have learned the basics, join a club, work with skilled trainers and hone your skills. Maybe then you can begin to dream of belting down a Highland burn in full flow, dodging the rocks.

39
Juggle

The more balls you juggle, the harder it is. Start with one ball and work your way up until you're ready to join a circus.

With one ball

■ Throw the ball in an arc from one hand to the other. Start with your hands at waist height and throw the ball up to eye level.

With two balls

■ Start with a ball in each hand. Throw the ball in your right hand up in the air.
■ When it reaches the highest point in the arc, throw the ball in your left hand in an arc to your right.
■ Catch the first ball, then the second. Pause, then repeat. Do the same exercise starting with your left hand instead of your right.

When you can juggle smoothly in either direction with two balls, you're ready for three.

With three balls

■ Start with two balls in one hand, one in the other. Assuming you are right-handed, it's easier to start with two in your right hand.
■ Start by throwing the ball in the front of your right hand in an arc towards your left hand.
■ When this ball reaches its highest point, throw the ball in your left hand in an arc towards your right.
■ Catch the first ball in your left hand.
■ When the ball from your left hand is at its height, throw the second ball from your right hand. This leaves your right hand free to catch the ball from the left.
■ When the second ball from your right hand is at its height, throw the ball in your left hand in an arc to your right, and so on.

It's a tricky skill and needs lots of practice. But once it's mastered it's a party trick for life.

40
Track an animal

1 Start early
The majority of mammals are at their most active at the beginning and at the end of the day, with only the larger ones making moves during the daytime. Early morning is often best to begin your tracking, as you don't want the light to fade halfway through your pursuit.

2 Find 'em near water
If you can locate a large source of fresh water like a river or lake, chances are this will also be the watering hole of the local wildlife. Most animals are creatures of habit and will frequent the same spot daily.

3 Follow tracks
Tracks are more prominent on wet ground. The age of a track on dry land can be determined by its moisture content. Has rain filled it? Is it cracked and hard? The clearer the impression, the more recently it has been made.

4 Food clues
Watch for partially eaten fruits, the gnawed shells of nuts, and remains of small mammals. Most animals are messy eaters and they don't clean up after themselves. The fresher the leftovers, the more recently your animal has been here. Keep an eye on the foliage around you – plant shoots and tree bark often bear the teeth marks of a hungry critter.

5 Dirty work
While it could easily put an end to your appetite, examining droppings left by an animal is the best way to determine what you're tracking. The bigger the load, the bigger the creature. And the drier the dropping, the longer it's been there.

41
Throw a Frisbee

When a Frisbee lands next to you on the beach, you want to be able to nonchalantly glide it back from whence it came – not spoon it into the family next to you. Here's how to throw a Frisbee straight:

- Backhand is easiest and most reliable. Stand sideways-on to your target with legs shoulder-width apart.
- Grip: place four fingers under the disc's rim with thumb on top. Hold the disc parallel to the ground throughout the throw.
- Cock your throwing arm by drawing it across your body away from your target.
- Now reach forward with your throwing arm to propel the disc towards the target.
- As you release the disc, flick your wrist to generate power.
- Time your release so the disc flies straight forward. Release too early and it will fly left of centre, hold on too long and it will go to the right.
- Follow through with your throwing arm. This will improve your accuracy.
- The disc should fly straight and true towards the chest area of the recipient.

42
Wash your hair without shampoo

Shampoos and soap strip your hair of the oils that keep it conditioned and tangle-free, so regular dunking in clean water is really all that's necessary for a healthy mop. But it can take months for the oils to be restored in hair that's previously been shampooed.

A weak vinegar solution will effectively deodorise and clean your hair – dilute one part with four parts water. A couple of spoonfuls of olive oil will restore shine, but be sure to rinse thoroughly.

43
Pass an exam

Exam pressure? British soldiers continue to study for and pass exams even when they are in places like Iraq and Afghanistan.

There's no better preparation for an exam than good old-fashioned revision. Study well in advance of your test – leaving it to the last minute will increase your stress levels and you'll struggle to recall information.

Avoid studying late into the night as this will disrupt your body clock and lead to poor performance. Equally, cut out caffeine, and sleep early the night before the exam. This will ensure you're bright and alert on the day.

Finally, quit any negative thinking. Doubting your ability will hinder your success, so think positive. Remember – you can do it!

1 Take all linen off the bed and lift up the mattress pad (if there is one) to give it a good shaking.

2 Lay out the sheet and pull it snugly over the corners of the mattress – you may have to lift up the last corner if it's a stretch. Smooth out the creases and tuck in tight along all four sides.

3 Spread the top sheet across the bed, going right up to the headboard, and begin by tucking in the bottom edge followed by the bottom corners. For a truly professional look, you'll need to do 'hospital corners' – this involves pulling the sheet tight from the side and folding the bottom-end overhang

underneath it. Then tuck in the side for a neat, vertical fold.

4 Place the blanket or duvet over the sheets, with its top edge about 20cm short of the headboard. Fold the upper part of the top sheet down over the blanket/duvet, then tuck in the sides of both. Some

people prefer to leave the sides untucked; anyway, don't make it too tight or you won't be able to get into bed.

5 Plump the pillows thoroughly before placing them on your freshly made bed. Lay the bedspread on top if you have one. Jump in for a snooze.

45
Survive at -30°C

At temperatures like -30°C, the cold seems to penetrate every fibre of your being. But there are ways to minimise its effect.

More layers, lighter clothes
It's generally better to have several layers of lightweight clothes on than one or two thicker layers – the gaps between layers serve to trap air, which can act as good insulation. It can also make it easier to move, and the more layers you have, the more you're likely to shield your body from unwanted moisture.

Protect your extremities
Frostbite is one of the biggest dangers. Fingers and toes need to be protected by thick gloves and waterproof boots. A lot of heat is lost through the head, so always wear a hat.

Protect your face
Not only can your face become badly exposed to frostbite, but the wind can make life difficult and visibility will suffer. Goggles are important, and you might wear a balaclava or consider sun screen if you're in an area where it's cold in summer – the ice doesn't half reflect the sun.

Find shelter
An igloo is one option (tip 188), but ideally you'll have an insulated tent. You'll want a butyl ground sheet, inflatable mattress and sheepskin, plus a double-insulated sleeping bag.

46
See in the dark

■ Your eyes are clever and will adapt to dark conditions. Be patient, it can be up to half an hour before they're 100 per cent adjusted – by which time they'll be 10,000 times more sensitive to light.

■ Look slightly to one side of whatever it is you're trying to view. There are no light-detecting 'rod' cells at the very centre of the retina, so in the dark you have a blind spot in the middle of your vision.

■ Close one eye when a vehicle passes or lights are flashed. This will ensure one eye retains good night capability and you won't bump into anything after the car has passed.

■ You might be able try the ninja trick of crouching low so your enemy/prey is silhouetted against the sky. But forget carrots – they do contain vitamin A, a lack of which can impair your night vision, but overdosing will NOT make it better than normal. That's a myth invented by British forces in WWII to put the Germans off the scent of radar.

47
Tread water

Maybe your plane ditched in the sea. Maybe the rest of your tropical diving team sailed off without you. Either way, you need to keep your head above water.

Being calm, relaxed and above sea level are your first goals. Get your lungs full of air, don't panic, and keep your breaths long and deep. Spread your arms out, palms flat, (as though you were sinking in quicksand). Slowly perform a wide breaststroke motion, wriggling like you're keeping a hula-hoop round your hips.

All the while, as your arms arc beneath the water's surface, kick your legs as if you're jogging underwater. Don't worry about coordinating your arms and legs — the important thing about staying afloat is feeling comfortable. Do what works best for your body and you'll still be breathing air when the rescue boat comes.

48
Survive a lightning storm

- Though there are people who have survived a dozen lightning strikes, one bolt can be enough to kill you.
- If you can hear thunder you are within range of a lightning strike.
- Count the seconds between the flash and the bang; dividing by five will tell you how many miles away the storm is.
- If you are in a group in the open stay 20 feet apart, as lightning runs through the ground after a strike.
- If you can't reach shelter, crouch on the ground (don't lie), feet together, head tucked in and hands off the floor. The places to avoid are underneath trees, tall metal structures (flagpoles, pylons) and small depressions in the ground (lightning could hit the ground and use you as a bridge). You are safer in a forest than beneath a lone tree.
- A car is a good temporary refuge but don't touch the metal sides.
- If inside a building, avoid touching metal or using the phone.

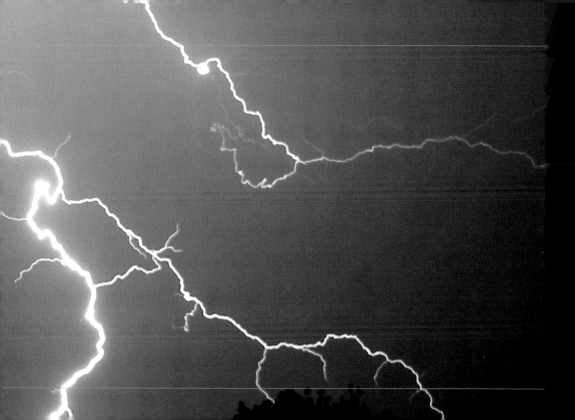

49
Knock down a wall

If you want to demolish a wall don't just wade in with your sledgehammer. First, determine whether it's a load-bearing wall. If it is, you'll need to find a way to support what's above – seek professional advice.

If working indoors, open the windows to let the dust escape and use protective masks and clothing. It's essential all electricity, gas and water are switched off before you begin any interior DIY work.

Begin small – use a crowbar to reveal what the wall is made of. Move on to your sledgehammer and work from the top down – if you start smashing at the bottom there's a risk it will collapse on top of you.

50
Eat an oak

1 If you are short on choices, an oak tree can deliver up a meal. First get a fire going under a pan of water.
2 Gather as many acorns as you can find and start boiling them – this gets rid of their tannin and makes them less bitter.
3 Re-boil in a fresh pan of water after an hour. Repeat this step four or five times.
4 Grind the acorns as fine as possible – the resulting powder is the basis for your dinner.
5 From this powdered acorn meal you can make bread, biscuits or even a cake.

Make a fire

A fire gives you heat, light, protection and the means to cook – all of which can be vital in the great outdoors.

Be prepared

Be prepared before you head out. Pack matches and lighters in waterproof bags. A sparkstick or a flint and a band of steel (or a knife) are a useful back-up if matches or lighter fail you. Cotton wool dipped in Vaseline makes excellent kindling.

Collect your wood

Gather twigs and branches of different sizes, the drier the better, and always collect more than you think you'll need (silver birch is good). If it's wet, take dead branches from trees rather than wood from the ground.

Light your kindling

Gather a pile of dry twigs and grass to use as kindling. Setting fire to your kindling is easy with matches or a lighter. If you have to revert to your flint and steel, hold the band of steel steady and strike downwards with the flint. Sparks will fly off. Repeat until the spark lights the kindling. In windy weather find a natural wind-breaker (eg cave) or position your body upwind of the fire to protect the flames.

Develop the fire

As the kindling catches light, blow gently to encourage the flames higher. As the fire takes hold, add some bigger twigs and small branches to the mixture of twigs and grass. Once these are burning, you can add larger pieces of wood. Build it up progressively.

If you don't want to be seen, digging your fire in to the earth will keep the light signature low. Digging it in will also allow it to stay lit in high winds and will concentrate the heat if you want something to boil quicker.

52
Fell a tree

- Look at the shape of the tree and work out which way it would naturally fall.
- Prepare an escape route at a 45° angle to the rear of the direction in which you expect the tree to fall.
- Cut out a wedge (with a chainsaw or axe) of a third of the diameter of the tree on the side you want it to fall.
- To fell the tree, start cutting horizontally about 10 centimetres above and directly behind the front wedge.
- Move away from the falling tree, letting the hinge assist in letting it drop. Shout 'Timber!'
- Put down your saw or axe and move along your escape route.

53
March in time

1 Technique

Marching is essentially over-emphasised walking. Arms, locked out at the elbow with fists clenched, are raised to shoulder height and then thrust back (producing a natural spring forward). The front leg makes a good stride forward. Head is held high and back remains straight. Marching is effective because everyone's moves are coordinated.

2 Get into a rhythm

The first step is the trickiest – get the timing and length just right and your body's natural sense of rhythm will take care of the rest. Soldiers use the instructor's command or, if marching to music, the downbeat to time their first footfall.

3 Practice makes perfect

It's important to listen to the drill instructor's commands and learn what they mean off by heart. Practise as often as possible.

54
Predict the weather

1 Red sky at night, shepherd's delight

It's not just a rhyme, there's science to it. A red sky at sunset is often a sign of a dry high-pressure system stirring dust into the air and moving towards you. 'Red sky in the morning, shepherd's warning' means that the high pressure has passed, trailing a less pleasant, moist low-pressure system in its wake.

2 Use your nose

In low pressure, plants release their waste. So a smell of compost may indicate that rain is coming in the near future. Swamps also release methane just before a storm, and flowers smell their strongest before rain. Wind can pick up at the start of a low pressure weather system, also indicating the possibility of rain.

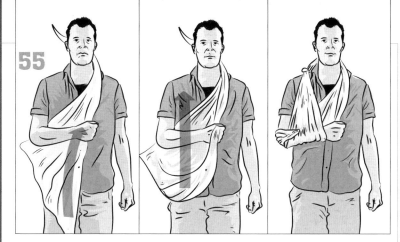

3 Look to the skies

A rainbow in the west means rain is heading your way – in the east it's already passed. Clouds are reasonably accurate indicators of weather. Cloud layers going in different directions usually mean bad weather is on the way, while clouds that look like fish scales mean rain within 36 hours.

4 Observe animals

If a storm is brewing, cows will huddle together and lie down. Flocks of birds flying low or sitting on power lines indicate bad weather. When those birds fly high, fair weather is on the way.

Make a sling

A sling provides support for a damaged arm and is quick and easy to make:

- Take a piece of material about one metre square.
- Fold it corner to corner so it forms a triangle.

- Place the middle tip of the triangle under the arm to be supported (this arm should be at right angles across the body), with the tip protruding slightly beyond the elbow.
- If you are supporting the right arm, place the top tip of the triangle over the left shoulder.
- Bring the bottom tip up over the arm and over the right shoulder.
- Tie the tips behind the neck.
- Pin the middle tip to the rest of the sling at the elbow.

56
Do the perfect sit-up

Method:
- Lie on your back with your knees bent.
- Your feet can be unsupported (as shown), or if you find it more comfortable you can hook them under something sturdy or get a training partner to hold them.
- With your hands crossed over your chest, use your abdominal muscles to raise your shoulders and trunk as if sitting up.
- When your trunk reaches a 45° angle, hold your position for a second and lower slowly but not all the way – your shoulders and head should not touch the floor.
- Raise yourself to begin your next sit-up.

Tips:
- Concentrate on good technique rather than speed – you'll get more benefit.
- Inhale as you sit up and exhale as you lower yourself. Don't hold your breath.
- Try to progressively increase the number of sit-ups you can do in a row each session.

Muscle groups worked:
Stomach, trunk

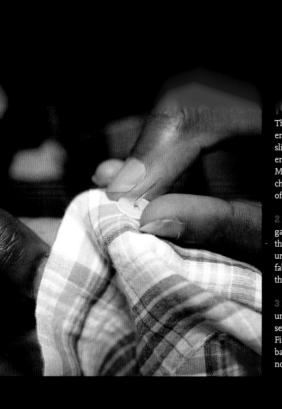

1 Cut your cotton to around 50cm. Thread the needle, then tie both ends of the cotton together and slide the needle along to the other end of your doubled-up thread. Make sure your knot is solid and chunky – tie another over the top of it if necessary.

2 Push the needle through the garment from the back and pull it through one of the button's holes until the knot jams against the fabric. Then push the needle back through one of the other holes.

3 Repeat step two up to eight times, until each hole in the button is secured by several double threads. Finish with a double knot at the back of the fabric. Trim the cotton no less than 5mm from the knot.

58
Pluck and gut a chicken

- Hang a freshly (and humanely) killed chicken upside down for an hour to allow any waste products to drain out of it. Then put it in a bowl of warm water for the plucking.
- Pull out the feathers in small clumps, being careful not to yank off swathes of skin (after all, that's the best bit). Once it's neatly plucked, cut the feet and head off and rinse it well, ready to be gutted.
- Locate its backside. Widen the opening a little with the help of a small incision. With the bird resting on its back, push your hand in, keeping your fingers on top, up against the breast bone. Go in as far as you can, and then curl your fingers down into the chicken's innards. Pull them out gently, being careful not to break the gall bladder.

59
Tickle a trout

A lot of people think the best way to tickle a trout is from the bank — it isn't. It's better to get into the water and find where they are hiding.

When resting, trout face upstream so water runs into their mouth and out of their gills. They rest up in the shade, often in a flowing clump of water weed or under a weir or bank overhang.

They live in clear, fast-flowing streams and rivers and can be readily seen from a bank or bridge.

Wear (old!) trainers and strip to shorts or swimming trunks, then walk slowly against the flow of water. When you come to a clump of weed feel gently through it with both hands, moving towards its base.

A trout in a clump of weed is already being tickled by the weed and enjoying it. If you touch one and it doesn't shoot away, use your fingers to gently tickle its sides and belly, moving one hand slowly forward to circle its neck. Keep the other hand around the body ahead of its tail, tickling gently.

A trout is surprisingly strong and slippery so be patient getting your hands into place. Seduce it, don't spook it. Once your hands are in position to grasp the fish, close them swiftly.

If you get it right you'll be able to lift it out of the water. If not, it'll wriggle free and be gone.

BE THE BEST...

Psyche out the opposition

Psyching out an opponent can gain you a crucial upper hand. It's often a simple case of confidence. Boxers who enter a ring oozing confidence, for example, will have the initial edge.

Maintaining eye contact is also a classic way to unnerve your opponent – it's a show of aggression, and an unblinking stare increases the intensity.

Purposely adding interruptions can also gain you the advantage. If you're playing cards, take a big gulp of water during your opponent's move and see how disruptive it is to their train of thought.

It's also crucial to know when to capitalise on your edge – if you smell blood, up your game and ram home your advantage. Oh, and never show fear, ever… unless you are bluffing.

61
Crack an egg
with one hand

TV and professional chefs don't just break eggs with one hand to show off – it saves time.

Hold the egg with all your fingers except your little one.

Crack it on a flat surface. Holding the egg, your thumb and index fingers either side of the crack in the egg and press to pull the egg apart. Not too hard, now.

Practise with both hands, so that you can eventually do two eggs at once. Apply for *Masterchef*.

62
Avoid a bear attack

If travelling through bear territory, you should call out every few minutes to scare off bears in the area – bears rarely look for confrontation. If you do see a bear, hold your arms above your head to make yourself look taller and talk to it softly. Don't run, back away slowly.

If a bear that feels threatened gets hold of you, you should lie still in a foetal position to show you're no threat. If it's a predatory bear seeking you out as food, however, you should make as much noise as possible and fight back to try to scare him off.

63
Lower your pulse rate

Snipers do it, magician Derren Brown does it on stage. But there's no great trick to lowering your pulse.

After taking your pulse, sit comfortably, relaxing your arms and your head. Take a deep breath and hold it until the count of ten. Then slowly exhale. Repeat this deep breathing exercise five more times. Measure your pulse rate again. It will have dropped.

It will rise again once you begin breathing regularly.

64
Deal with insect bites

Insect bites are often more irritating than dangerous, and most you can treat yourself.

Check the bite area for signs of the insect and remove any sting with a flat-edged surface like a credit card. Wash the area with soap and water and apply an ice pack or a towel soaked in water to reduce swelling.

You can make a soothing lotion using three measures of baking soda to one measure of water. Taking an anti-histamine tablet will reduce the reaction.

If you feel nausea, cramps or fever, or if your lips or throat become inflamed, seek emergency help immediately.

Throwing green foliage on a camp fire will repel mosquitoes if you're camping out.

65
Fight fire with fire

If you live in an area susceptible to forest fires during the drier months, you can protect your land by starting your own, controlled fire in calm, damp conditions around the area you wish to protect. This removes any combustible material from the path of any oncoming, out-of-control fire, and swerves it away from your plot. It's called a firebreak.

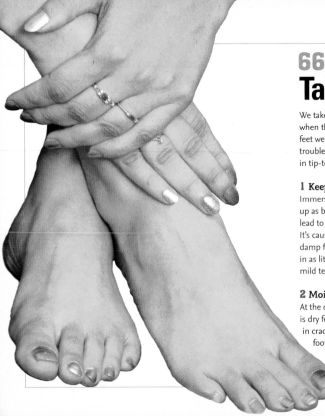

66
Take care of your feet

We take them for granted but when things go wrong with our feet we can end up in serious trouble. Here's how to keep them in tip-top nick:

1 Keep them warm and dry
Immersion (or trench) foot shows up as blisters or sores and can lead to gangrene if untreated. It's caused by wearing tight, damp footwear and can occur in as little as half a day, even in mild temperatures.

2 Moisturise
At the other end of the scale is dry feet, which can result in cracked, dry skin. Use a foot-specific moisturiser containing urea, after a going over with a pumice stone. Apply after the morning shower and before you go to bed.

3 Avoid fungal attack
A hot, itchy sensation between the toes could be a sign of athlete's foot, caused by a fungus infecting the skin. Apply a proprietary cream or powder to the affected areas following a shower (and clean the shower for the next person!). Athlete's foot thrives in warm, damp conditions so give your feet some fresh air.

4 Trim
Cut toenails straight across (not on the curve) on a regular basis to avoid the risk of an ingrowing toenail, further fungal infections… and holey socks!

Lay a brick

Brick basics

■ A 'stretcher' is a brick with its long side exposed (2in x 6in).
■ A 'header' shows its small side (2in x 3in).
■ The 'frog' is the indentation in the top of the brick.
■ A 'course' is one layer of bricks.
■ Different brick patterns, or 'bonds', are used on different walls.

The first brick

■ Scoop up a dollop of mortar on your trowel. Spread a one-inch thick layer about six inches wide on your foundation.
■ Place a brick onto this bed, frog up. Tap it down firmly with your trowel handle until the mortar layer is half an inch thick.

■ Use the edge of the trowel to slice away any excess mortar that has been pushed out below your brick.
■ Make sure the brick is straight and level.

Joining bricks

■ To join two adjacent bricks (eg two stretchers end-to-end), trowel three-quarters to one inch of mortar in the space where they will join.
■ Push them together to compress the mortar to about half an inch thick. Again, cut away any excess mortar.
■ To lay a brick on top of others, trowel a layer of mortar into the frog of the lower bricks. Lay the new brick on top and tap it into place using your trowel handle – the

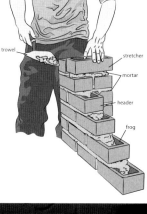

mortar should again be compressed to about half an inch.
■ As well as cutting away excess mortar, go back and brush the faces of the bricks with a 'foxtail' brush to wipe away excess mortar and smooth the joints.

Now you're ready to build a wall (tip 109). A wall requires planning and great attention to keep it level and straight.

68
Make a gas mask

You will need: a shower cap, a tin can, goggles, some wire net, two hankies, rubber bands, gaffer tape, some charcoal, some soda lime.

1 Fit the shower cap over your face and cut holes for the goggles, and a hole at mouth level for the tin can.

2 Remove the ends of the tin can. Wrap two parts charcoal to one part soda lime in the hankies. Put them in the can.

3 Cover the ends of the can with the wire net and join

to the shower cap with the gaffer tape. Make sure the goggles and the can are sealed to the shower cap with gaffer tape.

4 Attach the gas mask to your head with the rubber bands, and breathe easy.

■ *During the First World War, before gas masks were introduced or if soldiers didn't have any available, they used to put cloths over their faces that they had urinated on. This had some effect against chlorine gas attacks.*

69
Make a good cup of tea

This method will guarantee you a good cuppa. The *perfect* cup of tea, however, is a matter or personal taste so experiment with tea varieties, milk and sugar levels until you discover your ultimate brew.

■ Use a clean, de-scaled kettle (tip 215).
■ Boil fresh, cold water.
■ Warm up the pot with water just before the kettle boils.
■ Use good quality tea. Assam is considered a superior leaf.
■ Add one teaspoon of tea (or one teabag) for each drinker into the pot.
■ As soon as the water has boiled pour it into the warmed pot. Stir well and allow the tea to infuse for 3-4 minutes.
■ Pour your fresh milk into your mug FIRST (milk's taste declines if it is heated above 75°C). Don't use too much – the tea is the star, not the milk.
■ Pour the tea into the mug through a strainer.
■ Add white sugar if you like (as with milk, don't overdo it). You might try adding a slice of lemon or a sprig of mint.
■ Stir.
■ Sit back, sip back and enjoy. It's best for drinking when about 65°C.

70

Walk

Soldiers are world-champion walkers. Follow their lead and you won't waste your life waiting at bus-stops frowning at your watch – and you'll burn off plenty of calories too.

- Keep your head straight and look forward – not down at the floor.
- Allow your shoulders to relax and your arms to move easily. Tense arms and shoulders interrupt the walking action.
- Arms should be slightly bent, moving forward and back rather than across your body. This will help you walk faster. As you speed up, your arms will rise more, but should never go above 90° (ie not above your shoulders). Keep your hands relaxed and unclenched.
- Keep your back straight, except when going uphill when you need to lean forward.
- Your stomach should be held in and your chest open, with your ribs slightly forward.

- Extend your legs as you walk, almost as if they start at the waist rather than the groin.
- Bend your knees when striking the ground, but don't bend them too much.
- As you walk, your heel should strike the ground first and then you should push off with your toes and the ball of your foot.

71
Perform an Eskimo roll

Fig 1

Fig 2

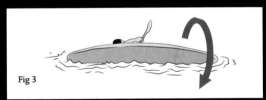

Fig 3

1 The Set-up
Climb into the kayak and attach the spray deck. Lean forward and to the right, holding the paddle on the right side of the kayak, as close to the water as you can get it, parallel to the water (fig 1). Capsize yourself to the right.

2 The Sweep
Keep your cool. Reach up to your right to break the water's surface with your paddle blades (fig 2). Then make a sweeping motion away from the boat – your left-hand blade should sweep through the water away from the kayak to gain purchase in the water, while your right-hand blade comes over the kayak hull. The momentum of the sweep starts the kayak rolling upright and brings your head and body towards the surface (fig 3).

3 The Snap
As the kayak starts to roll, straighten your body and continue the sweeping motion. Quickly snap your hip up and continue with the roll. Keeping your right knee and hip pressed against the underside of the deck will help your upper body to emerge from the water. Your head needs to be the last thing to surface.

4 Recovery
The forces of gravity on the kayak will pull you out of the water as the kayak rotates. Lean back as your kayak rights itself.

■ This is a risky manoeuvre so master it safely in a pool with a qualified instructor.

72
Hail a taxi

Catching a cab can be competitive. Make sure you get the edge.

■ In a side street or backwater? Find a bigger street or landmark where cabbies roam.

■ Scan the horizon for the tell-tale yellow light meaning a cab is up for hire. Scan both ways – cabbies will happily do a u-turn.

■ Spotted one? Make it yours. Move towards it, raise your arm, call out, step out slightly into the street (careful!), make eye contact with the driver as soon as possible.

■ Once it pulls over, move quickly and confidently to get inside. You could yet be gazumped. Tell the driver your destination and you're off.

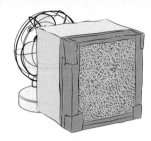

73
Make an air filter

You can make a basic air filter with a desk fan, its box, crushed charcoal and cloth.

■ Take the ends off the box and cover one end with a couple of sheets of cloth and seal them in place, leaving a bit of slack.
■ Stand the box on its open end, and distribute charcoal evenly on the sheet.
■ Stretch another couple of sheets over the charcoal and make the outer sheet as taut as possible and seal with gaffer tape.
■ Place the fan in the other end of the box, blowing inwards, and your rudimentary air filter with now be blowing filtered air.

74
Row a boat

■ Grip the oars firmly and, keeping the oar blades parallel to and just above the water, reach all the way forwards.

■ With a twist of the wrist turn the blade of the oar 90° forward and drop the oars into the water.

■ Gradually pull back, driving the blade through the water just below the surface.

■ When you have completed the stroke and are leaning back, lift the oars out of the water, twisting your wrists back so the blades are parallel with the water again.

■ Do not dip the oars too deep to start with. Rhythm is key and continuous gentle strokes will get you there more quickly and with less effort than big heavy strokes that send you in the wrong direction.

■ A firm foot rest is vital for power.

75
Polish silver

No-one polishes the posh stuff like a soldier. Here's how to get your own precious metal, from your best belt buckle to your football trophies, looking the business.

Rinse each item in hot water to get rid of any dirt and dust. Then, while the silver is still warm, dip a damp sponge or rag into your cream/polish and spread it all over. Taking a small area at a time, rub gently until it comes up gleaming.

Rinse again in cold running water, rubbing away any traces of polish with a clean soft rag. Dry thoroughly to avoid leaving water marks, using a towel that won't leave lint behind. You can use a cotton bud for tricky little nooks and crannies. Stand back and admire.

Thankfully, you shouldn't have to polish silver more than a couple of times a year.

76
Drive off-road

Simply pop your tank into first gear, point it at your destination and away you go… oh, sorry, you don't have a tank? In that case a 4x4 will have to do – and there aren't many places it won't go if you know how to get the best out of it.

- Before going off-road, get to know your vehicle on ordinary roads – having a feel for its dimensions and handling will come in handy later. Check the maximum water depth it can cross without flooding the air intake, and make sure the spare tyre is properly inflated.

- If off-road conditions are really muddy, deflate the tyres slightly for extra traction. Keep up a steady speed and stay in the higher gears as much as you can. When following a heavily rutted track, keep one wheel on the central hump to avoid damaging the underside of the car.

- Approach deep ditches diagonally so you don't have both front wheels going in at the same time. Cross fast-flowing water in the same way – a 45° angle upstream will help you to slice through the current.

- Approach steep climbs head-on. Power up in the highest gear you can, easing off just before you reach the summit. For descents, stay in first gear and don't use the brakes or accelerator if the ground is slippery – they'll send you into a skid.

- Aim to minimise your impact on the environment. Follow the trails or you could easily end up lost or stranded – and possibly in trouble with the law.

77
Abandon ship

- Assuming the worst – no life raft and no life jacket – tie knots at the bottom of your trousers before jumping overboard. The trapped air can help you float and save valuable energy. Avoid debris or other leapers when you jump.
- As soon as you're in the water, swim away from the ship fast – it will suck you down with it if you're too close.
- Once the boat is down, swim back to the wreckage area and salvage any food or anything that will help you float – a wooden door, a barrel, anything.
- Conserve energy by floating on your back and taking deep breaths. The more air there is in your lungs, the more buoyant you will be.
- Avoid any movements that speed your heart rate, as this leads to more heat loss. Move as little as possible.
- If you are lying in the water during the day, cover your head and neck with clothing to avoid sunstroke.
- If you're running out of water, fish are a good source of fluid as well as food. If you snap a fish in half, you can suck the water from its spine bones, as well as sucking its eyes.
- What you really want is help. Keep your eyes peeled and signal to any boat or plane or land you see.

78
Communicate using smoke signals

Using smoke to communicate is tricky and limited, which is why a standard set of signals has never been established. After all, if a standard signal meant 'we attack at dawn', then everyone would know – including the enemy. Native Americans used smoke frequently, but the meaning of the signals varied between tribes.

1 It's important for both the sender and receiver to work out what a certain pattern means in advance. A simple code might be one puff for 'safe', two puffs for 'caution' and three puffs for 'danger'.

2 Build your fire in an open area as high up as possible. This increases the distance the signal can be seen from. To get denser smoke, use grass and green sticks once the fire is going strongly. Signals can be seen a long way off.

3 To generate a puff of smoke, cover a fire with a blanket and remove it before it catches fire (wetting it helps). Variations in size, timing and shape of puff can be learned with practice, so more varied messages can be sent.

Live in a cave

Planning to hide out in a cave for some time? Whatever your reason, choose your location wisely.

Many caves are extremely damp, which is not good for the lungs. They're also dark and prone to rat infestation, so take an oil lamp and plenty of fuel.

Your cave should stay cool in the summer. Caves tend to have a constant temperature year-round. In the UK that is usually 13-15°C (in the mid to upper 50s°F), whereas in warmer climates it could be 19-20°C (66-68°F).

Make sure you come up for fresh air and sunlight at least once a day.

Caves won't have any facilities so you'll need to organise a makeshift toilet (tip 165) outside, well away from the cave.

Drinking water could be collected from a stream and purified by filtering (tip 197) and boiling it. Collect rainwater for washing or bathe in a nearby lake.

Unless there's a natural chimney within the cave, cook outside on a fire of wood. If you haven't taken supplies, you'll need to hunt for your food.

And take a pack of cards and a good book – you're going to get bored in there.

80
Build a pontoon bridge

1 Choose your site

A pontoon bridge is a temporary structure that floats on the surface of a body of water (usually a river to allow it to be crossed), rather than stretching above it and being permanently fixed like a conventional bridge. So you'll need to find a quiet stretch of river for your crossing point or run the risk of your floats – the 'pontoons' – being swept away during construction or afterwards.

2 Assemble your materials

You'll need: enough rope to reach from one bank to another; sufficient pontoons to support your surface all the way across; planking or other strong, flat material to form the surface of your bridge; and enough binding material to lash it all together. Pontoon bridges can range from simple affairs made of rope and barrels to more sturdy structures enabling many men and vehicles to cross (pictured).

3 Construct your bridge

String at least one rope from one bank to the other – this will be your guideline. Start positioning pontoons along the guideline, lashing each new one securely to the one before. Work outwards from both banks if possible. When you've assembled a continuous line, lay the surface and bind securely. Add a handrail if possible and the pontoon bridge is complete.

81
Track a yeti

The mythical yeti has been sighted as far north as Siberia and as far south as Indonesia, but your best bet has to be the Himalayas. The Khumbu region of Nepal seems to be the most likely spot – head for the Manju river and look out for gigantic footprints – up to 30cm (see tip 40 for how to track an animal). Then simply follow the yeti to his lair and shoot him… with a camera, of course. This is the 21st century.

82
Mend boots

■ Superglue will keep a detached sole in place for a short time. Make sure the glue has fully dried before wearing the boots again – that's vital, so read the glue label and be patient!

■ Duct tape makes a temporary patch for a hole. Use several layers, working from the inside.

■ For a waterproof solution, fashion a patch out of oilcloth or rubber – a tyre's inner tube is perfect – and duct tape it in place over the hole, again working from inside the boot.

■ If the hole is in the sole, slide something durable – card at the least – over the hole as well to fill the hole from the inside. Tape it in place.

Take a good photograph

1 Think about composition
Anyone can take a photo – taking a good one is a different matter. You need to add forethought to inspiration, and that starts with composition. Is there an ugly road sign to the left of the smiling couple? Then move your shot an inch to the right. If there is a car bonnet in the right hand side of your sunset shot, zoom in or pan away.

Don't always feel that the subject of your photo has to be in the middle. Dull photos can be easily improved with unusual angles and framing. Don't be afraid to experiment.

2 Make use of the light
Manoeuvre yourself around your light sources – if the sun's beating down, get your shot from an angle where it doesn't burn out your picture. If it's dark and you're using a flash, forget about close-ups and distance – a flash is only good for anything between two and ten metres away.

3 Relax your subjects
If you're taking pictures of people, help them relax. Take a variety of shots – some when they're saying cheese, some when they're off guard. You'll get a natural shot that way.

4 Liven up landscapes
If you're taking landscape photographs, remember: a big barren shot can come across as a little dull. Find an object that gives it a focal point and perspective, be it a pylon, a passing plane or a dynamic cloud on the horizon.

5 Be quick!
Sometimes, the best potential award-winning photographs exist in time for a millisecond, then they're gone. Don't hesitate – get the shot. Just remember to take the lens cap off first. With digital cameras, taking lots of shots doesn't cost you any more – you can edit out the bad ones later.

84
Give CPR

Cardiopulmonary resuscitation (CPR) is a technique used in emergency situations to assist heart attack victims. Though it is unlikely to actually restart the heart, it can keep the patient alive until professional help arrives.

The best way to learn this technique is to do a first-aid course. But even if you haven't been formally trained, you should attempt it if there is not a medical expert to hand.

If, after giving artificial respiration (tip 141), the patient still has no pulse, you will have to pump the blood you are oxygenating around his body. You must press the heart against the backbone to squash the heart and expel the blood from it.

Method:
- Place your middle finger where the patient's lowermost ribs meet the breastbone and your index finger above it on the lower breastbone. Place the heel of your other hand at the tip of that index finger.
- Place the heel of your first hand on top of the other and interlock your fingers.
- Lean over the patient with your arms straight and press down hard until you have depressed the breastbone by around 5cm. Release and repeat 15 times, alternating with two breaths of artificial respiration.

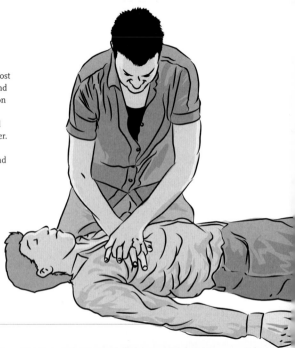

85

Peel 1000 spuds

- Use a proper peeler – it's far quicker than hacking at your spuds with a knife. Wind string around the handle to make a grip. After wetting the potato, try to remove the bulk of the skin in one go, like you would an apple. Top and tail the spud, and use the tip of the peeler to remove any eyes – 999 to go!
- For potatoes cooked and peeled in one, try the fire and ice method. Make a thin cut around the middle of the potato and boil for 20 minutes. Remove carefully and plunge it into ice water for 30 seconds. Then grip either end and the skin should part, like shelling a nut.
- Cheat – cook them skin-on. The skin's the most nutritious part of the spud, after all. Brush with oil, salt and pepper then bake for 90 minutes; chop roughly into 'rustic' style chips; or simply wash new potatoes and boil in their skins.

86
Stone a mango

To make a mango stone-free, take a sharp knife and core all the way around the circumference of the fruit, making sure that the knife blade makes contact with the stone at all times.

Clasp each end of the mango with both hands and give it a good hard twist. The mango will separate into two halves and you can pop the stone right out.

87
Shuffle cards

There's more than one way to shuffle cards. The easiest to learn is the 'overhand shuffle'.

1 Hold the deck at top and bottom with your left hand, positioning the deck on its edge. The fingers of your right hand rest lightly under the deck with your thumb on top of the deck.

2 Lift about half the deck up with your left hand, holding the rest of the cards back with the thumb of your right hand. You should now have half of the deck in each hand, with your left hand above the right.

3 Now move your right thumb out of the way as you lower your left hand, placing these cards from the bottom of the pack on the top of the pack.

4 Cover part of the deck with the thumb of your right hand again and lift up the other half of the deck with the left hand. Place the cards from the bottom on the top.

5 Repeat several times. You should now have a well-shuffled deck of cards. Square up the pack and deal.

88
Fix a leaking tap

1 Cut the supply
Turn off your mains water supply. Make sure the tap is turned fully on and put the plug into the plughole to prevent any small parts falling down the drain.

2 Unscrew the head
Unscrew or lever off the cover of the tap to reach the main screw. Remove this and the head of the tap should come clean off.

3 Loosen the main nut
Underneath the head is a large nut which will require a spanner to undo. If it's stiff, apply some vegetable oil and wait ten minutes. If it's really stiff

you could cause damage by exerting too much leverage.

4 Free the washer
Get your screwdriver and prise off the washer. There may be a small nut holding the washer in place so unscrew it with your spanner. Again, if it's particularly stiff to undo, add some vegetable oil and let it soak in.

5 Add a new washer and reassemble the tap
Get a new washer and replace the old one, adding a small amount of grease – Vaseline will do. Replace your tap parts in order, ensuring you tighten any nuts that came off.

89
Survive a swarm of bees

1 Don't swing your arms around wildly – you'll just make them angry.

2 Cover your face with your hands as much as possible.

3 Don't stand still. Decide on your escape route and run there quickly in a straight line.

4 A dive into water is the surest way of dislodging a whole swarm.

90
Stand completely still for two hours

Guardsmen have to stand still for long periods, ignoring rain, tourists and inquisitive insects. Here's how to do it.

1 Adopt the right position
There's an art to standing to attention. Stand straight and tall, chest lifted and shoulders squared. Rest your body weight equally on the balls and heels of your feet. Don't lock your knees or it might affect your blood circulation.

2 Manage your mind
Your brain needs to stay active. Find something to keep it busy: run over song lyrics in your mind, perform mental arithmetic, play word games, invent fantasy football teams…

3 Manage your body
The body isn't designed to keep this still for this long – even when asleep you toss and turn continually. To help avoid cramp, squeeze your fingers and toes and rock back and forth on your feet (slowly so nobody sees!).

4 Manage your time
Break the time up into smaller chunks. Twelve periods of 10 minutes are less of a challenge than two long hours.

Step 1

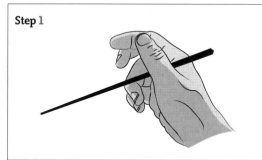

Step 2

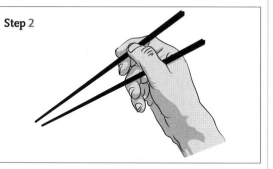

Step 3

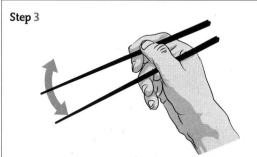

91
Use chopsticks

1 Place one chopstick between thumb and index finger, and rest it against the side of your (bent) ring finger.
2 Hold the other stick between the tips of the index and middle fingers, resting its thicker end against the base of the index finger and using the tip of the thumb to hold it in place.
3 Keep the first chopstick still and use your index and middle fingers to manipulate the upper one. Hold the bowl near you.

92
Do the perfect pull-up

Method:

- Stand underneath or facing a gymnastics pull-up bar.
- Grasp the bar with an underhand grip, arms straight and body vertical. Keep your back straight, shoulders relaxed and feet together.
- Using your arms, take your body weight and pull yourself up towards the bar smoothly.
- When your chest reaches the bar, pause for a moment before lowering yourself down slowly and in control. Don't straighten your arms completely.
- Lift your body back up to begin your next pull-up.

Tips:

- Inhale as you push up and exhale as you lower yourself.
- Don't hold your breath.
- Concentrate on good technique rather than speed – you'll get more benefit.
- Try to progressively increase the number of pull-ups you can do in a row each session.

Muscle groups worked:

Upper arms, shoulders, back, chest

93
Sit out a sandstorm

1 In a vehicle
First, try to outrun the storm. But the fastest storm can travel at 75mph, so if it's catching up make sure you park up before it reaches you – high-speed driving in bad visibility is very dangerous. Pull off the road, close all the windows, block any air vents and prepare to sit this one out.

2 On a camel
Camels are far better able to survive a sandstorm than you are, so have your beast sit down and use it as a windbreak. If you've got one, put on a mask, or wrap a moist cloth around your nose and mouth. A dab of Vaseline in the nostrils will help protect them from the whirling sand. Sunglasses will be nearly useless, but airtight goggles are good. Otherwise, wrap a cloth over your eyes.

3 On foot
If among sand dunes be careful to stay on the slopes rather than in a dip, as that's where sand will build up. Protect eyes, mouth and nostrils as above. Get to high ground if possible – there's less sand flying the higher you are – and never hunker down in a ditch, as there's a danger of flash flooding. Use any shelter you can, whether it's a boulder or your own backpack, then hope it's the over-in-minutes variety of storm rather than a two-day special…

94
Tell if someone is lying

Bad liars

Essentially you are looking for unusual behaviour, which betrays something they are not telling you. The most obvious signs are that they will avoid eye contact, might turn their head or body away and may fold their arms defensively. Look out for them touching their face a lot, maybe scratching their nose or ear – all tell-tale signs of lying.

Liars often speak more than normal as well, to avoid any awkward silences.

Good liars

To catch a seasoned fibber you're going to have to pay closer attention. Look for changes. This could even mean *more* eye contact than normal, or any difference in body language that reveals a change in thought patterns. A longer pause, a shorter pause; more arm movement, less arm movement; eyes darting down instead of up, or vice versa – all can be signs of a lie.

Try changing the subject. Liars may subconsciously relax if the topic changes because they feel less guilty. Watch for changes in their body position, facial expression and tone of voice that might give away their guilt. You have to look as closely as you listen.

95
Survive a snake bite

There are around 3000 species of poisonous snake in the world, but barely a **dozen** are considered dangerous **to** human life. **So** the odds on a fatal **bite are** slim.

To avoid being bitten, wear long trousers and whack the ground with a **stick as you walk. If you do** see a snake, **stand still and** it will **probably** slither away. Don't pick it up, even if it **looks dead.**

Different snakes **have different venom, and need** different **treatments. In** serpent-packed tropical areas, local medics will know the signs to look out for – but **the** principles of first aid are the same wherever you are:

1 Stay still and quickly wash the bite area with clean water.
2 Wrap a bandage firmly around the bite to stop the venom spreading – but don't make it so tight that it cuts off the blood supply completely.
3 Get to hospital as quickly as **possible.** Running is a bad **idea, and** you'll probably be feeling **faint and/or** sick at this point, so may **need help.**
4 Make sure the people **you** are with know to keep you **sitting up** or in the recovery position, otherwise you could choke on **your** own vomit.
5 Give doctors an accurate description of the snake. If you're in danger of passing out, **describe** it to someone else in your party first.

Use Morse code

Morse code is a communication system made up of combinations of dots (short units) and dashes (longer units) representing the letters of the alphabet. Learn 'SOS' if nothing more.

Send using light…
Flashing a torch or reflecting sunlight off a mirrored surface enables silent, line-of-sight communication over many miles in Morse. During the Vietnam War, captured American aviator Jeremiah Denton was able to blink the word 'torture' when he was paraded on TV by the North Vietnamese.

…or using sound
Morse adapts well to sound transmission, with a short interval between knocks corresponding to a 'dot' and a longer one to a 'dash'. People trapped underground, in buildings and in submarines have used Morse to communicate, as have prisoners by knocking on walls or along pipes.

Over the radio
Skilled operators can send Morse at up to 30 words per minute using an electronic 'key', but one of the system's great strengths is that you can simply squeeze the send button on a radio – say in a situation where you don't want to be overheard. Morse only takes up one-twentieth of the bandwidth needed to understand speech, so is vital in areas of poor reception or over long distances where there's signal noise.

A	·—	M	——	Y	—·——
B	—···	N	—·	Z	——··
C	—·—·	O	———	0	—————
D	—··	P	·——·	1	·————
E	·	Q	——·—	2	··———
F	··—·	R	·—·	3	···——
G	——·	S	···	4	····—
H	····	T	—	5	·····
I	··	U	··—	6	—····
J	·———	V	···—	7	——···
K	—·—	W	·——	8	———··
L	·—··	X	—··—	9	————·

Shout

1 Use your body

Lazy speakers only use air from the top of the lungs, but for effective shouting you'll need to employ your entire lung capacity and push air out by contracting your abdominal muscles and diaphragm (the sheet of muscle that stretches across the base of your rib cage).

This frees the upper-body muscles that power the vocal cords to concentrate on one job: SPEAKING VERY LOUDLY!

2 Strengthen the diaphragm

Lie on your back and place a heavy book just above your belly button. Breath in by expanding your diaphragm rather than your chest – the book will rise. Then blow the air out slowly without allowing the book to dip and let out an 'oooh' sound. Repeat this exercise often.

3 Stand correctly

To help your breathing, stand ramrod straight, feet shoulder-width apart with one slightly forward. With practice you can now combine full-lung breaths and diaphragm control to produce a deafening cry of "Ten — SHUN!"

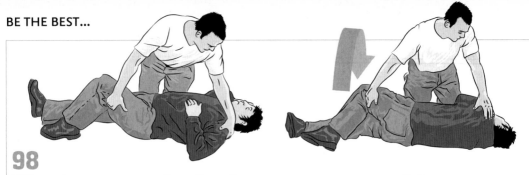

98
Place a casualty in the recovery position

The recovery position is a first aid life-saver. It allows a casualty to breathe freely and ensures they won't choke or stop breathing.

1 Kneeling next to the body, open the person's airway by tilting their head back and lifting their chin.

2 Straighten the person's legs and place the arm nearest to you on the ground at right angles to their body.

3 Pull their top arm across their chest and place the back of their hand against their top cheek.

4 Grasp the far leg above the knee and pull it towards you, keeping the foot on the ground.

5 Keep their hand pressed on their cheek and grip the top leg and roll them towards you and onto their side.

6 Tilt the head back to make sure they are breathing easily. Ensure the hip and the knee of the upper leg are bent at right angles.

7 Call 999 for an ambulance and stay with the casualty until the ambulance arrives, checking that they can breathe freely.

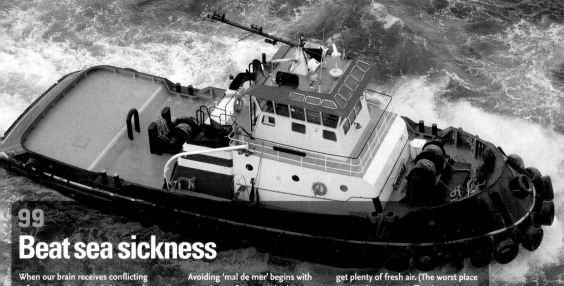

99
Beat sea sickness

When our brain receives conflicting information about our balance and body position the result is 'motion sickness', with symptoms of nausea and dizziness. Out at sea, this can be particularly unpleasant (and messy!).

Avoiding 'mal de mer' begins with getting plenty of rest and drinking lots of fluid – though not of the alcoholic variety. If you're on a ship move to the centre, where it tends to be more stable. Concentrate on the horizon and get plenty of fresh air. (The worst place you can be is in a stuffy cabin with no view of the horizon.)

If the above isn't working, try closing your eyes and lying down – relaxing is often a simple solution.

100
Wash your clothes in a river

- You can use soap as a detergent, or soak clothes overnight in a dilute vinegar solution...
- ...but more environmentally friendly is to simply soak them in clean river water. Beat the clothes on rocks (not sharp ones though) to get rid of stubborn stains. Repeat as necessary.
- Air-drying will get rid of smells, or hang them on the branches of a pine or spruce tree for that mountain conifer freshness.

101
Hand-sew a badge

If you want to make sure your badges don't budge you need to get to grips with the art of the backstitch:

The tools
Badges and insignia have thick backings, so you'll need a tough needle to pierce through them – ask for a 'size three sharp'. Use thread that's the same colour as the perimeter of the patch or, for an exquisite finish, ask for 'invisible' nylon thread.

The preparation
Lay your garment flat and carefully pin the badge in position. Measure enough thread to go twice around the badge's perimeter and thread your needle.

Starting off
From inside the garment, push the needle up and out, bringing the thread through the cloth and badge then back through to create your first stitch. Do four or five tightly overlapping stitches before pulling taut to

anchor the thread. Then you're off.

The stitching
Keeping your looped stitches neat, close together and as near to the perimeter as possible, work your way around the badge. Don't stitch outside the perimeter or your handiwork will show. When you return to your start point, finish off with several small stitches. Trim any loose threads. Relax and wear with pride.

1 Signal Brigade

4th Mechanised Brigade

16 Air Assault Brigade

12 Mechanised Brigade

11 Light Brigade

20th Armoured Brigade

102
Camp without a tent

A simple but effective outdoor shelter can be made using a waterproof sheet or tarpaulin with eyelets, some cord or rope and a groundsheet. Tent pegs are a bonus, otherwise you will need a knife.

1 Find two trees around 3m apart on a flat piece of ground (if you are in a forest, find a location at its edge). Check there are no loose or dead branches in the trees that could fall on you during the night.

2 If you don't have pegs, you'll need to make some. Find a branch about a finger thick, chop into pegs and sharpen. Cut a notch in them to secure your ropes.

3 Lay out the rope between the two trees, place the tarpaulin over it and then tie each end of the rope to the trees at chest height.

4 If you have guy ropes, attach them to the tarpaulin, pull tight and peg in. If you don't, secure the tarpaulin with logs or stones.

5 Place your groundsheet underneath your shelter and build a fire nearby (tip 51).

103
Put up a shelf

1 What your shelves are going to hold should determine what fixings you use. Use a cavity wall plug or, if your plasterboard wall is particularly weak, dry wall anchors (which should need no pre-drilling). Don't overload these.

Shelves for light objects can alternatively use a screw and toggle fixing, but heavier loads should be supported by brackets which attach to the studwork (lengths of wood) behind the plasterboard. You can use a stud detector to work out the positioning of the studs.

Don't drill into any wall until you've checked it for pipes and electrical cables. You can buy a cable and pipe detector to help you do this.

2 Use a pencil to mark up where the shelves are going to go, and use a spirit level to ensure the positions you mark for the fixing brackets are in the right place. Ensure the brackets are no further than 60cm apart in order to prevent sagging.

3 Ensuring your drill bit matches the size of the wall plug, drill the holes for the brackets to the depth of the wall plug. A good tip for getting the correct depth is to measure the wall plug against the drill bit and wrap some tape around the drill bit at that depth.

4 Screw the fixing brackets to the wall using screws at least two inches long and wall plugs at least 1.2 inches long. Ensure they grip firmly. Unless the shelves clip onto the fixing brackets, for stability they need to be attached with panel pins or screws.

104
Snowboard

1 Find an easy, wide slope. Attach your board's safety leash to your front leg (left leg if you are right-handed). An escaped snowboard can be lethal.

2 Fasten your front foot to the board, checking your heel is secure and your ankle strap tight, then your back foot.

3 Stand up at the edge of the slope. Apply a little pressure with your lead foot. Bend your knees and keep your back straight.

4 Your board will follow your body, so maintain control and balance by keeping your arms and hands extended along your sides and point in the direction you want to go.

5 Use your weight, not your legs, to steer, applying weight on the heel and toe edges to turn left and right or slow down.

6 If you fall, don't use your hands to break your fall. You might break your wrists. Roll as your body hits the powder instead.

"THE BOARD WILL FOLLOW YOUR BODY. KEEP YOUR BALANCE BY EXTENDING YOUR ARMS"

105
Negotiate a pay rise

First and foremost, do a good job. That's the most compelling argument there is for a pay rise.

You'll need a meeting with your manager. Before you set one up, make sure your work is up to date and up to scratch. You could even put in a few high-visibility late nights.

Begin the conversation with a calm and cordial outlining of your case in purely professional terms. Try to appear overworked but not stressed or unhappy. You won't get your manager on your side by whining and grovelling, but by emphasising positive aspects of your performance at work.

There's never a shortage of things that seem expensive – houses, child minders, golf clubs. Be persuasive yet friendly.

Only get tough if your boss gets tough first. Threats of leaving should be a weapon of last resort – especially if you're not prepared to have your bluff called.

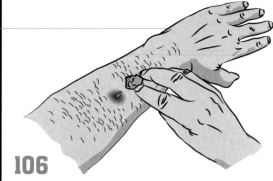

106
Get a parasite out of your body

One of the dangers of roughing it in the great outdoors is Mother Nature's love of symbiotic organisms. Parasites to you and me – little blighters that burrow under your skin and make a home of your body.

One good way of getting rid of these subcutaneous hitchhikers is to trick them with the promise of a good dinner. Locate the site of your infestation, and then place a piece of fresh meat over the area. The greedy parasite will head up towards the steak and start feasting on it. It's a bit like tempting the dog out of the kitchen by throwing a steak into the garden (only a bit more personal).

Conquer fear

The old saying about overcoming a fear by confronting it is true. And short of hypnotism or expensive psychotherapy, it's the only way that really works.

Fear is generally a good thing – after all, it's the fear of getting run over that stops us wandering out into busy roads. But if life is all about overcoming challenges, then we all need to face our phobias – that is, our irrational fears.

If you have a phobia of spiders, pick up a spider. Watch it scuttle across your hand. Have you passed out? Have you been infected with radioactive venom? No. And congratulations, you're no longer frightened of spiders.

Fear of something that actually is a tiny bit dangerous – for example a parachute jump – is more tricky. In these cases you need to stop yourself falling into a panicky spiral of 'what-ifs'.

Always talk to someone you trust about your deepest fears before the big moment comes. Then breathe deeply and slowly, sip water to stop your mouth drying up, and simply refuse to let your thoughts go into that dark place.

108
Drive across a swamp

1 Recce the route
Walk over the territory you're about to cross, noting which parts are particularly boggy. Always wade through water holes, checking the depth and for hidden hazards. After a thorough recce, plan the best route across the swampy terrain.

2 Select a gear
Choose a gear – second or third are better than first, which can generate too much wheel spin. Note the position of the steering wheel when the wheels are pointed dead ahead; if you're going straight when the wheel says you're turning, you're actually getting bogged down. Set your speed and stick to it – momentum is critical.

3 Troubleshooting
If you feel the vehicle sliding, reduce power until you get a grip. The same applies for wheel spin (moving the wheels side to side might help you regain traction). If bogged down, stop without braking and clamber out to take a look – you'll have until your vehicle sinks to the axles to work out a plan, whether that means reversing or digging yourself out.

Still stuck? Wait for a tow.

109
Build a wall

1 Bricklaying
Before you can think about a wall, first you must learn how to lay a good brick (tip 67).

2 Foundations
A wall one metre high needs foundations of half a metre. Fill the trench with concrete (sand, cement and gravel) and level it off.

3 Corners
Build the corners first and then work towards the centre. Run a length of string between one corner and another as a guide so you can keep your layers of bricks level.

4 Strength and bond
English bond, made up of alternating layers of stretchers and headers, is the strongest

bond for a one-brick thick wall. Flemish bond can also be used. (Important: a wall described as 'one brick thick' is the thickness of the LENGTH of a brick).

If you're building a simple 'one-skin' wall half a brick thick, the stretcher bond (laid end-to-end) is what you want.

5 Straightness
Keep checking straightness with a spirit level. It is impossible to make every brick totally straight, so only check the wall as a whole. Use a spirit level to ensure your wall is level.

6 Finish
To finish off, lay the last course of bricks with the frog (the grooved side) facing down so the smooth side is on top for a tidy finish.

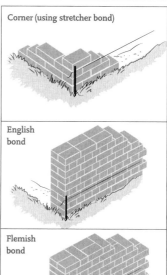

Corner (using stretcher bond)

English bond

Flemish bond

110
Throw a left hook

The left hook is often the most explosive punch in a boxer's armoury. Mike Tyson and Joe Frazier were among the finest exponents of the shot – here are the basics of throwing one:

Balance
Your back (right) foot stays put. All the manoeuvring will be done with your left, which needs to stand on its toes for flexibility.

Timing
Don't throw a left hook if you're under fire from a volley of jabs – the time it takes to manoeuvre will see you felled instantly. You must be up close to your sparring partner and have enough energy to make the punch count when you make contact.

Strike
When your opponent is weakened enough, get into position: right foot firm, left on its toes, body swinging to the left with your arm low, right hand guarding your face, left arm locked at a 90° angle, and swing from left to right, clocking your fellow boxer square on the chin. Get it right and they'll crumple.

111
Walk on your hands

Find somewhere with a soft and flat surface, so if you fall you'll have some padding. Ideally, have a 'spotter' (a friend) to help you.

■ Lift your arms straight above your head and lunge forward with one leg.

■ Lean forward, but keep your body straight, placing both hands on the floor. Kick up into a handstand.

■ Steady yourself for a few moments. Then lean to one side so your weight is borne by one hand.

■ Lift the other hand off the ground and move it forward. Take small 'steps' at first. You'll need to shift your whole bodyweight very slightly in the direction you intend to travel or you'll fall on the floor.

■ Now move your weight onto the hand you've just moved. Lift the other hand up and forwards and repeat. You're off and running – well, almost!

112
Reduce your stress

Stress tends to emerge when you don't feel on top of things. This doesn't necessarily mean you have more on your plate than you can actually cope with – it might just seem that way.

So being more organised, at work and in your home life, can make a big difference. Make a list of what needs doing and identify the priorities, then tick them off as you go. You may even find that the list is shorter than you expected. If the list turns out to be unrealistically long, you might simply have too much stuff in your life. Think seriously about giving up a commitment or two.

And talk to someone you can trust about how and why you're struggling – a problem shared is a problem halved, as they say.

If you work in an office, take regular screen-breaks. Always have a proper lunch-hour away from your desk, don't get into the habit of working beyond your paid hours, and be sure to take up all your holidays. It will make you a better employee.

Your secret weapon is setting aside a few quiet moments each day to do nothing, say nothing, and think about nothing. Find a space away from the noise and bustle, sit down, take some deep breaths and let your shoulder muscles relax. It's like a screen-break for the brain – and it can really help you keep your head straight and your stress down.

113
Survive a fall from a roof

Czech stewardess Vesna Vulovic once survived the drop from an aeroplane at 33,000ft. So how hard can it be to walk away from a fall off a roof?

1 Try to turn

If you have the time and agility, as you roll off the tiles twist your body so that you strike the

ground feet first. In the second (or fractions of) you're in mid-air, relax your muscles, bend your knees and try to land on the balls of your feet – these measures can lessen the force on impact thirtyfold.

2 Get ready to roll

Rolling helps even out the force of impact over more of your body, lessening the chance of serious injury. Twist your hips to roll sideways on impact; failing that, roll backwards. Don't roll onto your chest.

3 Anticipate the bounce

People have survived great falls, only to die when they bounced and landed badly a second time. Protect your head.

114
Avoid the runs on holiday

First of all, cross your fingers. The world is awash with bugs that your belly isn't used to, and you can't be sure of keeping them all out unless you holiday in a bubble.

You will improve your chances a lot by remembering that your worst enemy in tropical countries is water. Stick to the bottled stuff, and don't have ice in your drinks. Avoid salads if you don't know what they've been washed in – get your vitamins from cooked veg, and fruit that's still unpeeled when you buy it.

When visiting countries not renowned for refrigerated transport, don't eat seafood in inland areas. And don't be macho with curries and chilli dishes – the hotter the spices, the more likely they're being used to disguise dodgy meat.

115
Lace boots

To lace a boot so it stays laced, you should always begin at the bottom of the lace holes and work your way up.

Thread the lace through the two bottom eyeholes so you have two equal lengths to work with. Thread the left lace diagonally through the next eyehole up to the right; then cross the right lace over the left lace and through the next eyehole up on the left. Continue to lace up the boots in this criss-cross diagonal fashion.

Keep the lace firm but with a bit of give, and tie once at the top. If you have any extra lace wrap it firmly around the top of the boot and finish with a small, tight double bow.

116
Survive a shark attack

The rescue boat is a blip on the horizon, you've been treading water for hours (tip 47), and all of a sudden you see a fin slicing through the water. First response: stay calm. Sharks will instinctively make for the first thrashing object in their vicinity, and you don't want to be that object.

Keep your eye on the shark, anticipating flanking moves. Don't play dead – it'll make mincemeat out of you. Your best option is to appear as a threat. If it comes near, aim any attack at the nose or gills. Should it get close enough to bite, aim for the eyes. Don't be squeamish – punch and kick with all your might, it's you or him.

If a shark bites you, remain calm and keep fending it off. It may up its attack rate if you're wounded, so you must try to show it who's boss. Get out of the water as soon as you can, and get medical treatment. A shark bite will bleed profusely, and even minor wounds can become infected rapidly.

117

Signal to an aeroplane from a desert island

1 Be in the right place
Planes fly over mountainous territory from low ridges to higher ones, so if you're in the hills work out the likely approach path of any rescue aircraft and plan your signals accordingly. Look for a flat, visible area to make any ground signal. If none is available, build a structure on a ridge that will give an unusual, unmistakable silhouette. If you've been in a plane crash, don't wander too far from the site.

2 Set fires
If fuel is abundant, set a triangle of fires. Otherwise, keep firewood dry and ready to be lit if you detect a plane. Green wood will produce plenty of smoke – it's this that a pilot will see, rather than the fire itself. If on a beach, try to produce black smoke by burning tyres and other man-made material. Torching a tree works well, but don't start a forest fire.

"IF YOU'VE BEEN IN A PLANE CRASH, DON'T WANDER TOO FAR FROM THE SITE"

3 Signal

Use a heliograph to attract a pilot's attention (in other words, use something shiny to flash sunlight). Be careful not to dazzle any rescuer. If you know your Morse code (tip 96), send a message – 'SOS' is a distress call recognised throughout the world and is made up of three dots, three dashes and another three dots. Use wreckage panels, foliage (make sure you get plenty of contrast) or dig trenches (leave the earth banked up to increase the shadow effect) to spell out emergency signals on the ground. Wave bright-coloured clothing from a pole.

4 Help a helicopter land

Prepare a helicopter landing zone: clear a flat area up to 30m in diameter with a clear approach path. Mark it with an 'H' scratched into the ground.

118

Do the perfect squat

Method:
- Stand straight, feet shoulder-width apart and toes pointing slightly outwards.
- Cross your arms over your chest.
- Lower your body, bending your knees.
- Stop when your thighs are parallel to the ground and hold your position for a moment.
- Push back up to a standing position, straightening your legs.
- Lower your body to begin your next squat.

Tips:
- Keep your knees above your toes.
- Push your hips back as you lower yourself. Your spine must keep its natural curvature.
- Exhale as you lower yourself and inhale as you rise. Don't hold your breath.
- Concentrate on technique, not speed.
- Try to increase the number of squats you can do each session.

Muscle groups worked:
Thighs, hamstrings, lower back, calves, buttocks

119
Gut and prepare a fish

Fish can be (relatively!) easily caught in the wild, are abundant and full of nutrition. Here's how to prepare them for cooking:

1 Rinse off any slime and dirt in cold running water, then cut off all the fins and scrape off the scales if they're big enough to need it. Rinse the fish again.

2 Holding the fish by the tail, with its head facing away from you, cut all the way from the anal opening to the gills.

3 Now you should be able to pull out all the innards with your fingers. Once the fish is gut-free, give the flesh a thorough rinse. Cutting off the head and tail is optional – some people say the cheeks of certain larger species are the best bit.

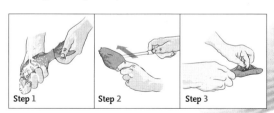

Step 1 Step 2 Step 3

120
Climb above a rainforest canopy

1 Conquer the trunk

A rainforest tree grows quickly and tall... very tall. Climbable, leafy branches aren't to be found until you're several hundred feet in the air. Although it's possible to ascend the clean, straight trunk using hooks, it's extremely dangerous. Modern botanists use cranes and even balloons to get up to the canopy.

2 In the canopy

Once you're up, the going gets a lot easier, with a dense network of sturdy branches to pick from. Keeping yourself roped to the trunk for safety, it should be easy to climb up and break through the canopy, which may only be 20-30ft in depth. Enjoy the view.

3 Set up a camp

The density of foliage, often interlocked with neighbouring trees, makes it possible to construct elaborate, permanent structures in the canopy. Treehouses connected by walkways and with rope chair-lifts to the forest floor have been occupied by scientists for months. And you can live on fruity monkey stew.

121
Play the drums

1 Hold the sticks loosely between thumb and index finger. They should be free to swish back and forth in your hands.

2 You need to train all four limbs to do different things at the same time. Get three of them up to speed with a basic 4/4 rhythm: start with a regular 'tiss-tiss-tiss-tiss' beat on the (closed) hi-hat, then introduce a kick-drum beat on the first beat of every bar (four hi-hat beats). Now bring in the snare on the third beat.

3 Start slowly, lifting the tempo a little once you're comfortable, before bringing the fourth limb into the equation by lifting the hi-hat for the beat just before the snare in every other bar.

4 Now you can start making things interesting. Start putting in light snare hits on the occasional off-beat (between hi-hat hits), then try switching from hi-hat to ride cymbal.

5 Once you've really locked down that groove, baby, start whacking the odd crash cymbal at the beginning of the bar, making sure you still hit the kick-drum at the same time. Now you can start trying out rolls and fills using the snare and the tom-toms.

Headstock

Nut

Tuners

12th fret

Bridge

122
Replace a broken guitar string

The Corps of Army Music boasts 850 soldiers, 23 bands and a wealth of musical talent and knowledge. Including how to replace a twanged g-string...

Before you bin the broken string, have a look at how it's secured. With most electric guitars this is a simple matter of passing it through a small hole from the back of the bridge or the reverse of the guitar's body. With steel-strung acoustics you need to pull out the plastic end-pin – making sure the little groove is facing towards the neck when you push it back in, as this is where the string's

ring-shaped end will rest against the bottom of the bridge.

Now pull the string fairly tight and give it two or three turns around the barrel of the tuner BEFORE threading it through the hole in the middle. This will save you some very tedious winding afterwards. Make sure your coils are neat, spiralling up from the bottom of the barrel to the hole, and above all make sure they're in the right direction: always curving outwards from the centre of the headstock.

Now kink the string 90° on its way out of the hole, and clip off the excess with

snub-nosed pliers. Ensuring the string is running over the correct saddle at the bridge, and the right nut-slot where neck meets headstock, tighten it up to pitch. In total it should go around the tuner's barrel no less than three times and no more than five.

Now it's time to put the poor instrument miles out of tune. Slip your fingertips under the string at the 12th fret and pull it a good few centimetres up from the fretboard. Repeat 10 times.

This stretching will leave the string horribly flat but, once you've brought it back in tune, it will stay that way.

123
Dress smartly

1 The basics
Looking smart is not about the latest designer labels or must-have item. A wardrobe containing the basics is enough: pressed trousers, a crisp cotton shirt, white T-shirts and a belt.

If buying jeans, go for a dark wash and a good fit. And once you find a look that works on you, buy it again and again in a number of colour variations.

2 Be comfortable
High fashion might look good on the peg, but won't look good if you don't feel right in it. Dressing for the terrain is essential here. A dark wool suit in humid conditions is the wrong choice.

3 Know your size
You might not be getting all your clothes tailored, but it's important to know your dimensions. Get measured up by someone who knows their way around a tape measure and you can buy clothes with confidence. Clothes that are too baggy look sloppy and careless, while clothes that are too tight can look ridiculous.

4 Coordinate
Smart people don't just throw anything on. There are times to contrast and there are times to complement. Learning what colours go with other colours is essential to be smart, and practice makes perfect.

124
Hoist a sail

In 2007 the Royal Corps of Signals – always up for a challenge – successfully sailed around the world in their yacht *Adventure* (pictured). Now you can't do that without hoisting a sail. Here's how to get that all-important wind-catcher in the air:

- Have your boat facing the wind and locate the halyard – this is the line which exits the top of the mast and which is attached to the head of the sail.

- Pull the halyard up and the sail will rise. As it rises, so the tension in the halyard will increase.

- Tie it a couple of times around the winch which is located near the base of the mast.

- Take hold of the winch handle and now you can raise or lower the sail by turning the handle clockwise or anti-clockwise.

125
Change a spark plug

Spark plugs should be changed every 30,000 miles on average. If your car has faulty plugs you will have trouble starting it. Buy new spark plugs with the right gap – see your manual.

1 Under the bonnet
Spark plugs are usually located in a row on top of the engine and will be attached to thick wires – plug leads. Bigger engines like the V6 or V8 usually have the plugs running along the side.

2 One at a time
Change one plug at a time to avoid mixing them up. Each fires in a specific order and if you mix the plug leads up your car will miss-fire and won't run at all sweetly.

3 Get a grip
Grip the plug lead as close to the plug as you can and slowly ease it off. By just grabbing the lead and ripping it off you risk pulling the lead apart.

4 Work it out
You'll need a special plug spanner or a wrench with an adapter to reach into the plug base and unscrew the old plug, turning anti-clockwise until it's loose. Take it out and clean around the edges of the fitting to remove any oil and dirt.

5 Good as new
With the new plug between your thumb and forefinger, slot it down into the plug hole and screw it in by hand to make sure it's correctly connected. Tighten with your spanner and click the plug lead back.

126
Defuse an argument

Understand that you won't 'win' or 'lose'
People rarely change their point of view just because of an exchange of words. So don't look at it like a competition. Let them have their say, and you have yours. Getting angry won't win you respect or agreement, it's more likely to have the opposite effect.

Take a deep breath, count to 10
It's a cliché, but that's because it works. Arguments escalate in the heat of the moment, and if you can control your own temper, you'll calm down the person you're arguing with.

Listen, don't interrupt
However outrageous the other person's words or actions are, you'll wind them up by not letting them have their say.

Think before you speak
If you blurt out the first thing you're thinking, chances are it could be something you'll later regret. Slow down your speech and look the other person in the eye, demonstrating that you respect what they are saying and they should respect your side of the argument in return.

Be prepared to apologise
Even if your words or actions have been misunderstood, apologise politely for not making yourself clear. Your apology may mean you'll get one in return.

If all else fails, walk away
If the situation is in danger of overheating, simply walk away and refuse to engage in confrontation.

127
Raise your IQ

The brain thrives on exercise – both mental and physical. Keep stretching your intellectual capacities with cryptic crosswords and sudoku puzzles, but don't forget to keep an eye on your general wellbeing too – get plenty of sleep, and go running or swimming.

Diet can also be a factor in intelligence. Keep well hydrated and go big on wholegrain cereals (including brown rice and wholewheat pasta), B vitamins (found in nuts and fish), iron (meat and fish) and fatty acids (fish, once again). If all else fails (or you don't like fish), just remember that anyone who brags about their high IQ is almost certainly lacking in the more meaningful quality known as emotional intelligence.

128
Chop onions without crying

Smeared make-up or bloodshot eyes are not a good look for a dinner party host.

How to thwart those onions? Chew on a slice of white bread while you chop. Sounds like an old wives' tale, but it does work. This doesn't just apply to bread, in fact – chewing anything (gum, sweets, whatever) can help.

When you're chopping onions, sulphuric enzymes fly out into the air and into your eyes, which try to wash the prickly enzymes away. Chewing forces you to breathe through your mouth rather than your nose, so the enzymes take longer to get to the eyes. Not as effective as wearing goggles, though. (But less ridiculous-looking.)

Another tip is to use red onions, which are less sulphuric than white.

You can also freeze your onions for ten minutes first, which slows down the chemical reaction once cut.

And avoid the centre of the onion too, because that's where the sulphur compound is most volatile.

129
Fall asleep on a plane

Keep yourself warm
Your brain associates warmth with rest and relaxation. Cover your arms and legs too, as that'll make it less likely that you'll be disturbed by the person next to you brushing you, and you won't feel the cold metal of the seat rests on your arms.

Use earplugs
Bring your own, as not all airlines provide earplugs for passengers. If you have no plugs, you'll find that running a tissue under a tap and rolling the resulting mush into a ball will make a makeshift plug that does the job.

Breathe deeply
Take longer breaths and slow your heartbeat, and you'll edge closer to the state of deep relaxation that is one step away from sleep. Imagine yourself sinking into your seat, as your body feels heavier, effectively hypnotising yourself into the land of nod.

Peace of mind
When trying to sleep, the last thing you want to think about is anything stressful. Make up a story in your head or drive an imaginary car round a track – with any luck, it'll edge you into a peaceful dreamland.

130
Reverse park

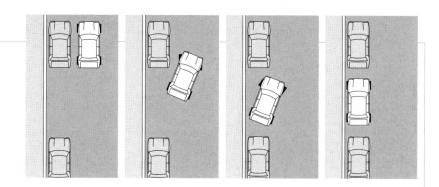

Reverse (or 'parallel') parking separates the assured drivers of the world from those who hold up traffic with embarrassing twelve-point manoeuvres. Once mastered, it's never forgotten.

Bumper to bumper
Sidle up alongside the car parked in front of the space you intend to slot into, with an arm's length from your wing-mirror to theirs. Your back bumpers should be neck-and-neck. The space you are aiming for needs to be at least 30cm longer (preferably more) than your car's length.

Mirror, signal, manoeuvre
Check your mirrors and make sure you're indicating towards the space. Once you're craning over your shoulder and pulling your front end into the road, the last thing you'll want is a number 39 bus ploughing into your bonnet.

Back it up
When you're clear, start backing up at low speed. Slow = success. As soon as your car starts inching backwards, turn the wheel as far as it'll go in the direction of the kerb. Once you've reversed to within 15-30cm of the pavement (check your mirrors) quickly begin turning the steering wheel fully away from the curb, swinging your front end into place as you ease into the gap.

Straighten out
Stop reversing when your back bumper is around 15cm from the car behind. Your nearside back wheel should not have hit the kerb! Then turn hard in the opposite direction and pull slowly forward, straightening up in the gap. You should end nicely in the parking space about 15cm from the kerb. Whistle nonchalantly as you get out.

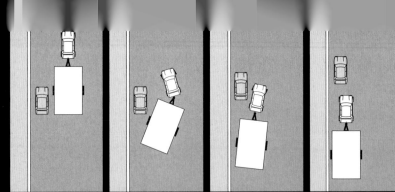

131
Reverse park with a caravan

Even the slickest parallel parker can come unstuck reverse parking with a caravan on the back of their motor. Keeping it slow and steady is the key.

Get help
Got a buddy? If so, get them to help. The parking spot you're aiming for has got to accommodate your car and your caravan, with a generous couple of feet to spare. If you have a companion who can get out and beckon you in, you're halfway there. If friendless, all is not lost.

Left is right
When you pull up alongside your desired space, you'll need a couple of feet between you and the car parallel to you, and the back of your trailer should be level with the back of said car.

Check mirrors, signal… it's time to move – slowly. This time, you're turning AWAY from the curb, because whichever way you turn, your caravan is going to go the OTHER way.

Slow and steady
As you reverse, keep your eyes on your mirrors and when you see the caravan slide into its space, it's time for you to turn the wheel toward the curb and slowly join it. As you do this, your caravan will move against your turn, so you have to keep the turns gentle and the pace glacial. As you manoeuvre frontwards and backwards, you should be able to jiggle you and your trailer into the gap. And just because you've done it once, don't think you won't need to practise till you're perfect.

Avoid a hangover

The short answer is, don't drink. If you are drinking, have the odd soft drink in between beers and make sure you eat as well as drink. But if it's too late for prevention and you need a cure, try this:

Drink lots of water
Before you go to bed, stagger to the tap and down two or three pints of water. Alcohol makes you dehydrated, so water will replace lost fluids and take the edge off your headache in the morning.

Eat well
The traditional post-session fry-up will help soak up any alcohol that's still in your stomach and give a much-needed energy boost. It's especially important to eat the next morning if you skipped a meal the night before.

Indulge your sweet tooth
Beer floods your body with sugar, the body produces chemicals to neutralise it, and so by morning your blood sugar will be low. Drinking a sugary soft drink or putting an extra spoonful in your morning cuppa will help bring sugar levels back to normal and make you feel more alert.

133
Tell a joke

Be funny

A lot of wannabe comedians out there forget that what keeps a comic on the stage is good material. If all you have are groan-inducing old chestnuts, all you'll get will be groans. If it's real laughs you want, remember your wits.

Be topical

It's the noughties, so gags about Spangles and Mrs Thatcher are out. Your audience doesn't have to be up on the latest current affairs to get your jokes, but at least make sure the frame of reference is fresh in people's minds. A stale joke will always stink.

Be sensible

Some comedians argue that as long as a joke is funny, it can't be offensive. That may be, but if you don't gauge your crowd's response you could find yourself a party pariah in no time. If you think you might cause untold offence, ask yourself if it's worth it. If the joke's so good you can't resist, you can't say we didn't warn you.

Be confident

Whether it's a shaggy dog story or a well-timed quip, the teller is in charge. To stay in charge, tell your joke at a measured speed, in a confident voice, and build up to the punchline in a timely manner. Don't get it in the wrong order, don't stutter the best lines – and don't smugly laugh along with your audience after the punchline.

134
Arm wrestle

Being strong in the arm might get you half way there in an arm wrestling contest, but weaker wrestlers can triumph by using winning techniques.

- If you wrestle with your right arm, position your right foot forwards.
- Get your body close to the table.
- Get a high grip on your opponent's hand.
- Raise your wrist to gain an advantage.
- Draw your opponent to your corner to open their arm.
- Turn your opponent's hand anti-clockwise, pulling it towards you. This is known as 'the hook'.
- Use the 'top roll', getting high up on an opponent's hand to put pressure on their fingers.

135
Survive in the desert

1 Seek shade
Get out of the sun. The intense heat will soon debilitate you, so find any shade going. Don't be tempted to strip off – sunburn and heatstroke can be fatal.

2 Find water
Finding water will be your number one priority, but don't attempt to dig in search for it – especially in the heat of the day. You'll use up more fluid in the exercise than you'll probably replenish. Seek out cacti and roots, as both will contain water (tip 03). Any animals you manage to catch are also a source of water – and you can suck the juice out of the eyes!

3 Don't waste energy
The heat will zap your strength and use up precious calories if you attempt a long hike without proper protection. You should only attempt to cover any serious distances at night when the temperatures are much cooler.

4 Eat carefully
Foods high in protein will speed up your metabolism, resulting in more water loss.

So try to eat only water-rich substances like plants and leaves. Resist going to the toilet because, again, you'll be losing more fluid that will need to be replaced.

5 Stay warm at night
While the days can be extremely hot, temperatures can plunge to near freezing at night. Keep hold of every scrap of clothing to keep warm after the sun goes down, and get a fire going if materials allow (tip 51). The extremes in temperature result in condensation forming in the mornings. If you have a plastic bag or container to hand, tie it tightly around any vegetation to help trap the morning dew.

136
Darn a sock

- Slide a light bulb or beer bottle into your sock – it will stretch the hole and keep the needle from getting snagged.
- Trim any ragged edges to the hole, then double-thread a darning needle. Don't wait for the hole to get too big!
- Work your way around the edge of the hole with a series of 3mm circular stitches. Overlap the start of your stitches to anchor the thread.
- Now sew a series of long, parallel stitches across the hole, inserting the needle each time outside the circle of stitches.
- Turn the sock 90° and make a series of stitches across the hole.
- Finish off by anchoring the thread with a couple of short, interlocking stitches. Do not use a knot, either to start or finish with – you'll feel it as soon as you wear your mended socks.

137
Build a solar power unit

The sun is the greatest power source available to man. And with the right kit it's quite simple to harness its energy.

First off, you need to focus the sun's rays. Set up a series of mirrors to channel its light to one central point. At this central point, have some sort of metallic element, preferably liquid sodium (this holds the energy longest), for the rays to heat. Above this element place what you want to heat, say a kettle. As the sun's rays combine to heat the element, the water will heat and eventually boil and you can enjoy a cuppa. Taking this idea a step further, you can use the steam created by boiling water to drive a turbine, thus generating electricity.

138
Plan a camping trip

A great camping trip will be remembered as an idyllic tryst with nature bathed in peace and birdsong. A bad one will be remembered as cold, miserable and drowned in argument. So plan ahead.

- Check weather forecasts before you embark on your trip. Do you really want nothing more than a tent to protect you from gale force winds? Even if the predicted weather sounds fine, take waterproofs just in case.
- If you plan on roughing it in the wilderness, a heavy duty sleeping bag and provisions for making a fire are recommended.
- Make sure you thoroughly map out where you're going, especially if it's off the beaten track. Is it public land? Will there be easy access? You may have to get permission from landowners to camp in some places, so do your research before you leave.

- Bring entertainment. After a few hours in the woods or a field, you might at least want to read, have a drink or strum a guitar.
- If you're roughing it, take any tools you will need. A knife will help you in all kinds of situations.
- Finally, ensure the area where you plan to camp has something worth going to look at, or nearby activities. There's no point camping between a quarry and a motorway. You can incorporate hiking, taking in spectacular views, boating, anything you like, with a little forward planning.

Essentials:

Seasonal clothing	Water
Shelter (eg tent)	Camping stove
Sleeping bag	Matches
Food supplies	First aid kit

139
Sing

- Never hold your breath. Fill the lower part of your lungs with air, as if you had an inner tube round your waist you were constantly filling. Most voice coaches agree that the diaphragm and controlling it is the single most important element in improving your singing. Good airflow and breathing means you can concentrate on the singing.
- Record your singing and listen to it objectively. What you hear in your own ears when you are singing can be very misleading.
- Hear the note in your head before you sing it. Don't guess the pitch.
- Open your mouth wider. Drink plenty of water.
- Sing with confidence. Nothing is more cringe-inducing than a wallflower on the stage.

140
Make a battery from fruit

Stuck without electricity? Have an abundance of fruit, some metal and wire? Then you can make a battery.

Take a piece of fruit and insert two 'electrodes' of differing metals (a coin and a nail will work fine) into it. Then run a wire from each electrode to the contacts of what you need to power and there you have it – you've made an electric battery.

One lemon won't generate much electricity, but you can run them in sequence, and have enough power for a lamp or a clock.

141
Perform artificial respiration

Otherwise known as 'the kiss of life', this is the fastest and most effective way to save someone's life if they are not breathing. It's essential first aid.

1 Check the patient's airway is not blocked by his tongue or vomit. While looking in the mouth, look along the chest to see if it is rising. Do these checks for ten seconds before confirming the patient is not breathing.

2 If he isn't, and there's no obstruction in the mouth, lie the patient back and tilt his head right back so his tongue lifts from the back of the throat.

3 Hold his jaw open and pinch his nostrils.

4 Blow deeply into his mouth until you see his chest rise. It should take two seconds for full inflation. Remove your lips and let his chest

fall fully (this should take about four seconds).

5 Repeat this once and then check his pulse. If his pulse is there, continue breathing into his lungs and check his pulse after every ten breaths. If breathing returns, put the patient in the recovery position (tip 98).

6 After two artificial ventilations if there is no pulse, the heart has stopped and you must pump oxygen round his body by compressing his heart. Proceed to CPR (tip 84).

7 If there are signs of recovery (coughing, colour returning etc) put the patient in the recovery position.

8 Hand over to a medical professional at the first opportunity.

142
Land a parachute

■ Fix the landing ground (drop zone or DZ) and any landmarks in your mind and ensure you always know where it is.

■ Your jump master will have told you wind speed and direction before you jumped, but continue to pay attention to the wind. Sudden gusts can prove confusing and speed your rate of forward or backward motion.

■ Pulling down on the left or right rigging will steer you in the same direction.

■ The closer you get to the ground, the faster it will rise up to meet you ('ground-rush'). So make sure you are in the right location. In the ideal landing you drop vertically onto the ground with little or no forward motion. To do this, turn into the wind as the ground approaches.

■ The golden rule is to keep your legs and

feet together with knees slightly bent. As you touch the ground, absorb the impact with your knees fully bent. Move into the parachute roll, easing your leg, thigh and bum to the ground, rolling over around your bum – it's padded and designed to cushion you.

■ Gather in your parachute quickly or it may drag you across the ground if the wind catches it.

143
Weld

Welding takes a lot of practice to do well, and it can be dangerous so don't be an impatient learner. The advice below won't make you an instant expert, but it should be enough to get you off to a solid start.

First of all you need to be properly equipped – safety glasses, thick leather welding gloves, steel-toe boots and a proper welding hood are essential.

You will make mistakes, so begin by practising on scrap metal. All surfaces to be welded need to be clean and rust-free – smooth them down with an angle-grinder if necessary.

Hold the torch at a steady angle with both hands, and move along the join at an even pace, welding in a tight zig-zag formation. If you're in doubt – and in danger of damaging something valuable – don't be too proud to call in a professional for help. You'll be glad you did.

144
Train a dog

The Army takes in hundreds of dogs, many with behavioural problems. But even a misbehaving older dog can be taught new tricks.

1 Choose a reward system
To encourage good behaviour, reward your dog with snacks, petting, praise or even clicks from a hand-held sound-maker. Once you've settled on a system, stick to it. And try to ignore bad behaviour rather than correct your dog.

2 Don't repeat yourself
Saying a command over and over only encourages your dog to ignore it, so don't repeat yourself endlessly. Give your dog three chances – *ask* it to do something, *tell* it to and then *make* it. Reward compliance promptly. Be consistent with both your commands and rewards. If your dog has 'learned' bad behaviour, such as barking, find situations where you actually want it to bark, then reward it.

3 Don't give up
Dogs get tired and bored, just like people, so keep sessions short – you can achieve more in three five-minute periods than one 15-minute one. Be patient, and remember that older dogs are happier to fit into a 'pecking order' (with you at the top!) than puppies.

145
Make a fish hook

From your kitbag
Any sort of pin, needle or safety pin can be bent into a fish hook. Needles have the advantage of an eye to tie your line to. Check the seams of your rucksack to see if they've been stiffened with wire: extract, bend and sharpen.

From man-made objects
Barbed wire is basically hooks on a string – use wire-cutters to snip off as many as you like. Nails or tacks can be hidden inside bait and, if swallowed whole, will do the job.

From the environment
Whittle dried hardwood into hooks, complete with barbed tips for extra deadliness. Look for twigs that are already the right 'V' shape. Tight lines…

146
Mend a puncture

What you'll need:
a puncture repair kit (consisting of patches, sandpaper, glue and a marker), a bicycle pump, tyre levers, a spanner to remove the wheel nuts (unless you've got quick-release wheels).

■ Stand the bike upside down and remove the wheel either with the quick-release or a spanner. If it can't fit past the brake blocks, release the remaining air in it.

■ If the cause of the puncture is visible – eg broken glass or a tack – remove it. Next, insert a tyre lever between the tyre and the rim, bend the lever back and attach to the spokes. Do the same with the other lever a couple of inches further down the tyre. If possible, slide the lever around the rim to lift the tyre away, or reposition the first lever and pry away again until the tyre is freed.

■ Remove the inner tube and find the hole. You may be able to hear the air escaping, or you can submerge it in water and watch for bubbles (if it is totally flat, inflate it a bit). Once you've located the puncture, mark it with chalk.

■ Use sandpaper to roughen the area around the puncture, then cover the area with adhesive. Allow this to go tacky and place the repair patch over it. Hold in place for at least five minutes. Inflate the tyre a bit to check the puncture has been fixed.

■ Put the tyre and slightly inflated tube back on the wheel (you'll need to work round the rim gradually tucking in the tyre, using the levers to help you). Inflate the repaired tube and then get on your bike.

Carve meat

- When the meat is cooked, take it out of the oven, cover it with foil and let it stand for about 20 minutes (or longer for a large joint). The meat finishes cooking and relaxes, and you will lose succulent juices if you carve it too soon.

- Ensure you have a good sharp knife, a steady surface and a carving fork to steady the meat.

- Ask your guests if they would like thin or thick slices of meat.

- Your knife should saw through the meat, not changing angle once it has made the first cut.

- Always cut across the grain. Find the grain by looking closely for tiny thin lines running along the flesh.

- The rarer the meat the easier it is to carve. The tenderest meat is often closest to the bone. And the tastiest!

148
Treat heat stroke

1 Spot the symptoms

A victim will appear disorientated and complain of dizziness, headaches and nausea. Their skin will be hot and red, their heartbeat and respiration fast. Take a temperature: 40.5°C/104°F or over and it's heat stroke.

2 Immediate treatment

Get the patient into shade and remove most of their clothing. Elevate their feet, fan them down and soak in cool water. As long as they're conscious, give them plenty of liquid to drink – sports drinks ideally. If you've got the luxury of ice packs, apply these to the armpits, palms and soles of the feet.

3 Keep monitoring

The victim's internal temperature regulation will have gone haywire, so be careful that your treatment doesn't shock them into hypothermia. Keep taking their temperature and, once it reaches 39°C/102°F or lower, stop with the water and/or ice. Get them to hospital, even if they appear to be better.

Prevention tips

- Stay out of the sun at the hottest times of the day; indoors ideally, if not in the shade.
- Drink plenty of water before setting out and throughout the day.
- Don't exert yourself under a hot sun; if you are active, take frequent breaks.
- Wear lightweight, loose-fitting clothing, plus a sunhat.

149
Change a car wheel

Safety first
As soon as you realise the need to change a wheel, get the car on a firm, flat surface away from the danger of passing traffic – never take a risk with nearby cars. Apply the handbrake and check the spare is blown up.

Jacking it up
Before jacking the car, lever the hubcap off and loosen all the wheel nuts with a wheel brace. Turn the nuts anti-clockwise until they can be undone with the fingers. Insert the jack in a jacking slot or under a firm part

of the chassis near the flat tyre. Jack the car off the ground.

Swapping the wheels
Take all the nuts off, keeping them safe in the hubcap. Pull the wheel off. Ensure the car is jacked up high enough to get the

inflated spare on. Put the spare on. Finger-tighten all the nuts, turning them clockwise. Lower the jack and tighten all the nuts with the wheel brace.

Now drive to the nearest garage to get the spare tyre repaired or replaced.

150
Surf

1 Lying on your chest, paddle the board to where the waves are breaking. Look over your shoulder for a wave and paddle your board in anticipation (with the front crawl) when a good wave is around five metres behind you.

2 Your intention is to keep the board in perfect 'trim' – balanced and under your control, supported by the speed of the wave.

3 As your board catches the wave and starts to accelerate its tail will lift up. Give yourself an extra boost with three power strokes then grab the rails of your board and lift yourself up on to your toes, planting your lead foot centrally on the board. Your back foot rests near the fins of your board.

4 When your feet are in position, release your hands and stand up.

5 Use your feet to distribute your weight evenly, keeping the tip of the board up, but not so much that your tail sinks.

6 To turn, tip in the direction of choice, lightening your back foot to let the board pivot. Surf's up!

■ **If you can't swim, don't attempt to surf!**

Tell the time by the sun

1 Rise and set

You'll need to have an idea of the times of sunrise and sunset for this to work. Let's say the sun rises at 6am and sets at 6pm (that's roughly average) with the sun at its highest point halfway through at noon.

2 Mark off the sky

Using landmarks on the ground, plot the course of the sun through the sky for an hour or two. Then estimate its entire arc over the course of the day and divide that arc into quarters (see left). Each quarter represents three hours of the day. So if the

sun's in the first quarter, it's between 6am and 9am. If it's two-thirds of the way through that quarter, it's 8am.

3 Get your timing right

Remember, the accuracy of your timing depends on having a good idea of the times of sunrise and sunset. You'll have to adjust those times depending on the time of year and your location: in London, for example, the earliest sunrise of the year is around 4.45am, the latest sunset 9.20pm. Use a book of tables to find sunrise and sunset times where you are

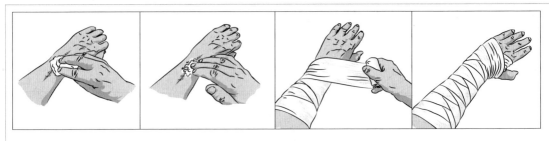

152
Bandage a wound

Out in the field, cleaning and bandaging a wound quickly reduces scarring, the chances of infection, and speeds up healing. What's the best way to do it?

Be clean
Your hands should be as clean as possible before handling a wound. If you can, disinfect them and wear latex gloves. The wound needs to be cleaned thoroughly and any visible debris removed (tip 257). Remove jewellery near the injury, as this can impede blood flow once swelling kicks in.

Get it under wraps
Apply antibiotic ointment to the inside of the dressing before putting it loosely on the wound. The dressing should extend an inch or so beyond the wounded area so that it can be affixed to uninjured skin. Secure the dressing with a clean bandage.

The winding of the bandage depends where the injury is: wrap it snugly but not too tightly to reduce the risk of swelling. If bandaging an arm, hand, foot or leg, leave fingers or toes visible so they can be checked for swelling.

153
Iron a shirt perfectly

1 Start with the collar. Flatten it out and iron from the point to the middle.

2 Iron the yoke by placing one shoulder and then the other over the narrow end of the ironing board.

3 Working down from the shoulder, iron the sleeves, creating a neat crease on either side.

4 Open the cuffs and iron them flat.

5 Slip the shirt over the board and iron the back.

6 Iron the front of the shirt, one half at a time.

7 Put the shirt on a hanger, buttoning the first and third buttons, and allow to cool.

154
Prevent and treat blisters

Blisters are caused by friction, heat and damp. Most commonly afflicting the feet, the best way to avoid them is to wear proper fitting shoes and ensure your heel does not slip when you walk. Avoid cotton socks – wool mix is best – and keep a spare pair with you.

Use talcum powder on areas where blisters occur and wear waterproof footwear if facing the elements. Small blisters can usually be left alone – simply cover with an elastoplast. If the blister contains a large amount of fluid, clean it with soap and water and insert the tip of a sterilised needle at the base of the blister. Let the fluid drain out, apply an antibiotic ointment and cover with gauze.

155
Appreciate art

Taking the time to drink in the beauty of a painting or sculpture is like a detox shot for the mind and the soul. Art is for everyone, and everyone can 'get it'. Not convinced? Wouldn't know where to begin in a gallery? Read on.

The Impressionists are a good place to start because they're accessible but not too hung up on the subject matter. Don't be distracted by what a painting is 'of'.

Focus on the way the different shapes and blocks of colour have been arranged, the use of light, and the texture of the paint itself.

Impressionist art can be very atmospheric, but just as important is the way the paintings are balanced. There'll often be one or two strong foreground elements that draw you into the centre of the canvas, and a dramatic background (or sky) that holds you there. Relax and let yourself be sucked in. After that, go with the flow and see what else floats your boat.

Of course, if you just want to bluff it in order to impress people, you'll need some names to drop. Your best high-brow bets are Vermeer (for composition), Matisse (for colour) and Titian (for just about anything).

156
Hypnotise a chicken

It can be done. Carefully pick up your chicken and tuck its head under one wing, then rock it gently from side to side.

After just a few seconds, you'll be able to set the bird down on the ground – very delicately – and it will be frozen in a trance for around half a minute. You'll wonder how you ever managed without this skill.

157
Play the bagpipes

The personal piper to the Queen plays under her window every morning for fifteen minutes. To get to this level takes much practice and there is an old Highland belief that it takes seven years to make a piper.

The Highland bagpipes consist of an airtight bag (often made of animal skin), a blowpipe to fill it, a chanter (the melody pipe) and three drones (that produce the distinctive continuous droning sound).

The secret is to fill the bag using the blowpipe so that the pressure is strong enough to close the valve that stops air rushing back down your windpipe.

The reservoir of air in the bag is then squeezed through the chanter and the reeds so you can have a breather from the blowpipe. Be warned – maintaining a steady flow of air is difficult and needs much practice. We recommend you start with a practice chanter.

158
Leave a secret message

In plain sight

If you've invented a secret code, you can leave messages out in the open. Pictograms like the 'hobo code' – symbols scrawled by tramps around towns in Depression-era America letting fellow tramps know things such as whether hobos were welcome in the neighbourhood, if a certain house had a guard dog etc – convey plenty of information in only a few lines. Or you can assign phrases to letter groupings – just using sets of three letters gives you 17,576 combinations to play with.

Out of sight

The enemy might not be able to understand your plain-sight messages, but they can destroy or tamper with them. But a hidden message should remain intact, and can even be written in plain text. You'll need to devise a 'message left' sign, however. In the field, a distinctive pile of stones might direct the recipient to search in a hole in the nearest tree. In the city, an innocuous chalk mark could direct you to look under a hedge or behind a street sign.

Combine the two

For maximum security, prepare hidden messages in code. Insert pre-determined phrases or combinations – always include three consecutive words beginning with the same letter, for example – so that if the enemy breaks the code and tries to falsify a message, you'll be able to tell because they won't have included the pre-agreed phrase or the tell-tale combination that shows it is genuine. Beware 'substitution' codes ('E' for 'A', and so on) – they're easy to break

BE THE BEST...

Lark's head knot

159
Make a hammock

You can make a simple hammock relatively quickly and easily. All you need is two ropes around 6ft long, a piece of strong material at least 8ft x 3ft and two sturdy supports (trees are ideal).

1 Knot the material – Tie a large knot in each end of the material.

2 Tie the rope to the material – Tie the two pieces of rope to either end of the knotted hammock using a lark's head knot (see insets).

3 Tie the ropes to the trees – Tie one rope securely around a tree about 7-8ft up the trunk (just above where two branches connect to the trunk for extra strength). Tie the second rope around another tree about 10ft from the first.

4 Enjoy – Hop in and doze off.

160
Skip

Skipping isn't just for children – ask any boxer. Skipping is a big part of their training – it's a great calorie burner, aids coordination and footwork, tones muscle and provides a cardiovascular workout.

Step 1
Choose a rope that's about the same length as your height.

Step 2
Hold the rope by the ends, with the loop behind your back at your feet.

Step 3
Throw it over your head and, without stopping, jump as it meets your feet.

Simple?
Well, keep repeating it until your timing is spot-on and then slowly increase your pace. Boxers aim to do three-minute skipping sessions – mimicking the length of a fight round. Work up from three one-minute sessions first.

When that's mastered, try alternating the rope under one foot at a time – a harder skill that will enhance your timing.

161
Be a good mate

Humans are social creatures, and therefore rely on interaction with their fellows to get through life unscathed. That's why we need friends – people we can rely on, who'll help us out in a fix. But friendships need work, and if you want a buddy who'll watch your back, you'd better be prepared to watch his.

Be loyal
If you're a true mate of someone's, never bad-mouth them behind their back. Never spill their secrets. And if you hear them getting bad-mouthed, defend their honour. Even if you can imagine what's being said might be true – they're your pal so stick by them.

Be a guardian
If you can see your mate's about to hit some trouble, look out for them. If they're about to drink and drive, take away the keys. If they're making some dreadful career/love life/personal decisions, take time to chat with them about what they're about to mess up. They'll thank you later.

Be there
We all go through hard times, have bad days, need words of encouragement. Take the time to have a drink with a pal when they're in need, be prepared to sit and listen to their woes when they need you to – you never know when you might need the same in return.

162
Swim butterfly

Butterfly is probably the hardest stroke in swimming. It's physically demanding and technically difficult. But it's pretty impressive if you can master it.

Head and feet
Timing is essential – while the head is out of the water, the feet should be kicking under the water, pushing the swimmer forwards. As the head slides under, the feet come up until the soles are out of the water. The feet then press down on the water, pushing the head upward again.

Arms and shoulders
The arms follow the movement of the head. As the head goes under the water, both arms should follow, scooping back under water and describing a keyhole shape from the shoulders to the hip. As the head comes out of the water the arms are thrown forward either side of the body to begin the stroke again. A cinch, eh?

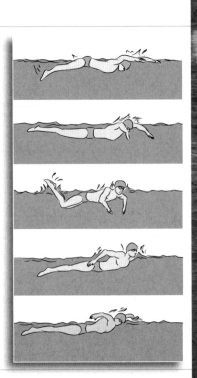

163
Remove a red wine stain

The secret to cleaning this notorious stain is to act quickly.

On a shirt
- Go to the bathroom and wash the red stain out. If that is not possible, blot the stain with damp paper towels or a clean damp cloth.
- Don't rub it or the stain will spread.
- If you have white wine to hand, cover the red wine stain with white wine. This will remove the colour. Then rinse with water, or sponge with a damp cloth.
- Machine-wash the garment as soon as you can.

On dry clean items
- Sponge the stain with damp paper towels or a clean damp cloth, removing as much of the colour as possible.
- Get the garment dry cleaned promptly.

On carpets
- Soak up as much as possible with tissues or a clean cloth.
- White wine or clear vinegar may remove the remaining red colour.
- If not, scrub with warm water and a mild washing-up liquid.

164
Apply cam cream

A pack of camouflage cream (known in the Army as cam cream) is standard issue for every soldier. It dulls the shine of the skin and allows soldiers to blend in with the natural environment when they're operating outdoors.

Cam cream comes in two colours – green and brown – and is applied to the face, neck and hands. You can buy it at many outdoor clothing shops.

The trick is to firstly apply a base layer (the brown cream) all over your face before breaking this up by adding different coloured random stripes on top of that. Be sure to apply the cream unevenly to blend in with the vegetation. To get the perfect look, dunk your fingers in the cream before dragging them over your face.

Remember not to overdo it with either colour – too much can make you just as visible as too little. Green men only exist in films.

If you don't have access to cam cream, mix a little water and soil together to make a mud mask. As with the cream, you should rub the mud unevenly over any exposed skin.

Keep reapplying the camouflage throughout the day as it can smudge and rub off.

To create the perfect 'invisible' look, combine your new make-up skills with some well-placed foliage (tip 203).

165
Dig a latrine

If you're camping out, when nature calls you need to build a decent latrine before you answer.

1 Location
Pick a spot a good distance away from your camp and make sure it's downhill. Don't choose anywhere near a water supply such as a stream or river.

2 Construction
Dig a trench about a metre and a quarter deep and place some rocks around the edge of the trench. Rest logs across the top, leaving a hole large enough to sit over comfortably. Fill any gaps with soil.

3 Make a lid
You'll need to make a lid to cover the hole as it's important the latrine is covered when not in use. Use a smaller piece of wood or a large leaf held down with rocks. This will help keep out flies and prevent smells.

4 Cover with soil
After each use, add a shovelful of soil. Don't add a disinfectant as this will kill the bacteria needed to break down the waste and will result in smells.

5 Keep moving
After a while the latrine will inevitably start to smell. Fill it in with earth and build a new one using new wood for the cover. Burn the old timbers to prevent spreading infections.

166
Kitesurf

You must be a good kite pilot before attempting kitesurfing, so practice flying your kite and controlling its speed on dry land first. You'll also need to know how to swim before trying this.

First, learn how to body drag. Get in the sea and use your kite to plane your body through the water. This way you can get a real feel for your kite before going on to use a board.

Now you are ready to kitesurf. With the wind at your back and the board in front of you, dive your kite to create power and lift you out of the water.

Keep your eyes on the kite, not the board, and keep your balance.

BE THE BEST...

167
Do a J-turn

The J-turn is a 180° spin done in reverse. It is highly dangerous, so don't ever attempt it. Leave it to the professionals, like stunt drivers and the Army's 'close protection' soldiers, who guard royalty and VIPs. Here's how they do it:

Start reversing
Begin reversing, looking over your shoulder all the way, and get up to a speed of around 25mph.

Kill your speed
Take your foot off the accelerator as fast as possible, no need to be smooth about it. This is what builds up the momentum for the spin. Don't forget to hold on to your breakfast.

Crank the wheel
Jerk the wheel in a full circle to the right (if you want to make a left turn). The car will start to turn into the spin. At this point, get your foot on the clutch and grab hold of the gearstick.

Straighten up, drive off
In one fluid motion, slam the clutch down, shift into neutral, clutch out, clutch down, and shift into first gear. The weight of the engine revolves the front end of the car like a pendulum, and as it completes the arc you'll need to straighten your front wheels. You'll now be facing forward and be ready to get on the gas and go.

168
Remove chewing gum

Gum in your hair? In your carpet? On your jeans? No sweat – try one of these tactics:

- Get an ice cube or a bag of frozen peas and hold it against the gum until the gum hardens. Chip away with a knife until it's all gone. If that doesn't get it all out, heat the gum with a lighter so it goes all gooey again, then re-freeze. You'll have it out in no time (not recommended for hair!).

- Rub a small amount of peanut butter into the gum (this works particularly well when it's stuck in hair), then let it sit for a few minutes. Then gently pull the gum/butter combo out until it's gone – no need for

snipping! There isn't a scientist on Earth who will tell you why this works, but it does.

- Apply the tiniest amount of WD-40 to the gum, watch it chemically break down, and then tweezer it off damn quickly. And get whatever item of clothing you've just put oil on into a washing machine as soon as possible.

169
Eat a posh meal

1 Know your napkin
Once seated, place your napkin on your lap and use it for occasionally wiping your lips or fingers. At the end of the meal, leave it loosely and tidily on your table mat.

2 Don't dip
If being served soup, don't be tempted to dip any bread into it, and neither should you mop up your plate with bread once you're finished. You may tip the bowl away from you to get the last mouthfuls.

3 Outside in
The traditional place setting of cutlery has the forks on the left and knives and starter spoons on the right, with the desert spoon and fork on top. The silver is placed in order of use for each course being served. In other words, begin at the outside and work in towards the plate.

3 Knife and fork
Hold the knife and fork with the handles in the palm of the hand, forefinger on top, and thumb underneath. If taking a break between mouthfuls, rest the knife and fork on either side of the plate. Don't put your elbows on the table. When you are finished, cutlery should be left crossed on the plate with the fork prongs pointing downwards over the knife blade.

5 Giving thanks
Always thank the host and hostess for their hospitality before leaving. Don't even think about asking for a doggy bag.

170
Lie

Telling a lie or a half-truth is on rare occasions the best option. Soldiers under interrogation might need to, for example (but don't try it with your mum, teacher, wife etc!). Lie-detector machines pick up on changes in heart rate caused by stress; shrewd people can spot the outward signs in the same way. The key to pulling off a proper whopper is to make the lie *feel* like the truth.

Tell it to yourself so many times, and with such conviction, that you actually start to believe it. Relax your way into the lie – if you worry too much about disguising it, you'll stress yourself out and your body language will give the game away.

171
Use hand signals

What it means: **Come to me.**
Why do it: **It's perfect for
gathering a group of individuals
together when you can't shout –
think getting the family together
at Alton Towers. Soldiers use it to
communicate orders discreetly.**
How to perform it: **Raise your left
arm and touch the top of your
head with your thumb and
fingertips, making sure your palm
doesn't touch your hair.**

What it means: **Stop. Don't move.
Stay where you are.**
Why do it: **Your shouts might be
drowned out in a commotion and
there are times when one more
step could mean disaster.**
How to perform it: **Extend
your left arm directly out
from your shoulder. Your
arm should be bent 90°
at the elbow, fingers pointing
up. Your palm should be open
and facing forwards.**

What it means: **Proceed in
single file.**
Why do it: **Essential when
negotiating tight streets, alleys
and riverbeds – or weaving your
way through a packed pub.**
How to perform it: **Keeping your
right arm by your side, raise your
left arm straight above your head
palm open, fingers pointing
towards the sky.**

DID YOU KNOW: **All these signals are performed with the left hand because soldiers hold their rifles in
their right hand. You can perform these moves with either arm!**

Ollie a skateboard

An ollie, named after its inventor, Alan 'Ollie' Gelfand, is when a skateboarder jumps into the air, seemingly with the board stuck to their feet. It's the building block for more complex and difficult skateboarding tricks. The ollie isn't a move for absolute beginners, though, so it's best practised once comfortable with basic skateboard riding.

- Place the ball of your back foot on the tail of your skateboard. Place your front foot between the middle of the board and the front trucks.
- Bend your knees deeply. The more you bend, the higher the ollie will be.
- Then slam your back foot down on the tail of your skateboard as hard as you can. At that moment, jump into the air, pushing off with your back foot.
- As you jump into the air you should roll your front foot inwards slightly and use it to guide the board through the air by dragging the side of your shoe forward along the board.
- When you are as high in the air as you will go, flatten out the skateboard underneath you. Make both feet level on the top of the skateboard.
- As you come back down to earth, bend your knees to absorb the shock of landing. Land front-foot first.

173
Skim a stone

Choose the right stone
Find a flat, smooth stone that fits comfortably into the palm of your hand. A common mistake is to discard heavier stones for fear they will sink, but some weight will add height and distance to your skim.

Master the technique
Your stone needs to hit the water at speed and at the acutest angle possible. Adopt a stance similar to a baseball pitcher, with your knees bent and non-throwing shoulder pointing at the water. The lower you can get, the better – aim to release the stone between ankle and knee-height. Concentrate on that flat trajectory.

The throw
Pick your spot on the water and throw the stone as fast and low as you can. Flick your wrist as you release the stone to add extra momentum and spin that will help the stone bounce. Now get counting (and practising) – the world record is over 50 bounces!

Did you know?
The World Stone Skimming Championships are held every year in Scotland. The competition is judged on distance rather than the number of bounces, but each stone must bounce at least three times. Fancy a shot at the title? To stand a chance of winning you'll need to throw well over 50 metres!

174
Make friends

When you're in the Army you're meeting new people all the time and becoming buddies. Not everyone gets the chance to make mates so easily, so here are some tips…

Join a club or team
A sports team or a club (which can cover anything from stamp collecting to bee keeping) is a great way to make friends. It even sparks friendships between people who have little else in common. The same goes for volunteering – it shows that you're unselfish, which makes you a more attractive friend.

Introduce yourself early
Being the quiet guy at the back won't help – let people know who you are as soon as possible. Remember people's names and use them in conversation – it tells them you're listening and fixes their name in your mind.

Master small talk
People don't want to get too deep and serious with new acquaintances, so make sure you've got a good line in inoffensive patter (tip 24).

Be positive
Try to smile, maintain eye contact and listen. Try not to interrupt too much or attempt to trump whatever story they've just told you.

Be trustworthy
How do you turn an acquaintance into a friend? By being reliable. If you've promised them something, deliver. If you are meeting, be there on time. If you've borrowed something, give it back promptly. These small steps build trust. Once you've made a friend, be a good friend (tip 161).

175
Disguise yourself

When the Groucho Marx glasses/ nose/moustache combo just isn't enough, and plastic surgery is a step too far, the art of disguise is all about being thorough. Much depends on where you are and who you're hiding from, but the first rule is to blend in with the people around you.

Change everything that can be changed: hairstyle, hair colour (including eyebrows), beard/ moustache (not so useful for women), skin tone (using make-up), glasses or contact lenses (tinted), and of course every last item of clothing from head to toe. Altering the profile of your clothes can make you look considerably thinner or fatter, as any fashion follower will tell you.

Don't just act it, live it. Practise changing the character of your voice, not just the accent, and learn to move in a different way – for example a slower walk or a less rigid stance. But don't go overboard with props (umbrellas, crutches, guide dogs etc) – most people don't carry any, and 'most people' is what you're aiming to look like.

If you have the physique to pull it off, there's also the option of dressing up as a member of the opposite sex.

Speed read

1 Ditch the distractions
How often have you ended up reading the same passage of a book three times because your mind keeps wandering off? Turn off the telly and radio, put earplugs in if necessary, and give the text your full attention.

2 Skim and search
Look for the words that jump out and grab your attention – these will most likely be the ideas you're most interested in. Slow down and read these parts fully, but then skim through the rest. Chances are the stuff in between is dispensable if time is of the essence.

3 Use a helping hand
It's easy to lose your place on the page, so by reading with your hand under the line you're on, moving it down quickly as you go, you will focus your eyes on the right line.

4 Don't read to yourself
Most people 'vocalise' what they're reading – ie, read it to themselves, sometimes actually moving their lips unconsciously as they're doing so. This will slow you down, as it means you're not just reading the words but repeating them.

5 Learn to read in blocks
Although you're taught to read word-by-word as a child, you usually read several words at a time, and with practice you can learn to extend the amount of words you read in each 'block', to the point where you're taking in a whole sentence or even a short paragraph at a time.

6 Practise
The more you read, bearing these tips in mind, the easier and faster you'll find it. You'll take in more information at speed.

177
Address the Queen

If you are introduced to Her Majesty the Queen, bow (tip 227) or curtsy (tip 250). Shake hands if she proffers hers. Address her first as 'Your Majesty' and thereafter as 'Ma'am' (to rhyme with Pam, not palm). She will control the conversation.

Drive a speedboat

There's nothing like the rush of wind and water as you drive a speedboat. To begin with, familiarise yourself with the controls, especially the onboard and cockpit lights, windscreen wipers and the bilge pump (which is used to pump out water taken on board).

The clutch usually has a release trigger under the throttle handle, allowing you to push it into gear. The further you push the throttle handle forward, the faster you'll go.

The steering works just like a car, except when in reverse when the nose of the boat will follow the direction you steer in. When parking on a jetty, ease in – unless you want match wood everywhere.

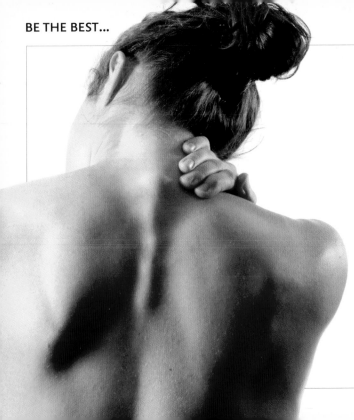

179
Massage yourself

The most popular parts of the body for massage are a bit of a stretch if you're doing it yourself. But you can do some light work on the head and shoulders.

For the head, stretch out the fingers of both hands as if to catch a football and, working your way around the scalp, manipulate the skin with short, quick movements of the fingertips – a bit like scratching yourself, except that the skin of the scalp moves with the fingers. This can be really de-stressing.

For the shoulders, rest your elbow on the arm of your chair so the shoulder muscles relax and manipulate vigorously between the fingers and thumb of the other hand. Give it a couple of minutes each side, but don't overdo it.

A few drops of unscented oil (eg: almond or grapeseed) will help reduce the friction.

Tame a lion

How do you tame a 250kg carnivore? You don't wait until it weighs a quarter of a tonne. It's essential to establish a bond while it's still a cub. Here's how:

- Don't raise your hands to fend off the playful attack of a cub. It will take this as a sign you want to play, and will continue this behaviour into adulthood. You don't want a play fight with an adult lion. A firm 'no' is enough.
- Have a spray of vinegar water or dog repellent to hand at all times. If the lion's behaviour gets out of hand, a quick blast will startle them. They will associate the bad behaviour with the 'punishment'.
- Keep a toy with you. If the lion starts to behave aggressively towards you, throw the toy away to draw the animal's attention away from you.
- Train more than one lion. Lions are sociable creatures and will be happier in company.
- Don't let your lion get hungry. A well-fed lion will be quieter and more obedient.
- Remember, you are in charge. If you want to tame a lion you have to turn into a lion yourself.

181
Peel an orange in one

Here's how to peel an orange without making a mess of the fruit or your trousers.

- Hold an orange in one hand and a knife in the other hand.
- Slide the blade of the knife horizontally into the top of the orange just under the skin.
- Rotate the orange with one hand while holding the knife

steady with the other, pulling the knife gently towards your body in a diagonal motion to create a spiralled, curling orange peel.
- Keep the width of the peel large enough so that it will remain in one piece.
- When you reach the other end of the orange, pull the peel away in one long curl.

182
Windsurf

The world speed record for a sailing craft is held by a windsurfer. The basics of this exhilarating sport can be learned in just a few hours if you join a club.

- Manoeuvre your board downwind, mount it and gain balance, with the sail in the water. Raise yourself up on your feet, holding on to the sail uphaul (a length of cord).

- Bend your knees slightly and pull the sail up using the uphaul, keeping your back straight.

- Place one hand on the mast and your lower hand on the boom (the

hand rail you grip to control the windsurfer) so the mast is leading the sail towards the bow (front end) of the board. When ready, transfer your other hand to the boom. The wind will set you in motion.

- The mast should be perpendicular to the board so lean back and keep your arms straight to keep it up, your body forming a figure 7.

- Pull with the hand nearest the back of the board to accelerate and let it out to slow down. Keep your feet behind the foot of the mast and your front foot forwards.

Sail

Mast

Uphaul

Boom

Foot strap

183
Roll up a sleeping bag

Sleeping bags come in different shapes and sizes but with most designs the principles are the same. Lay the bag completely flat and try to push out as much air as possible as you zip it up. Then fold it once lengthways so it's no wider than the depth of the sack, and roll it up slowly from the bottom – very, very tightly. Keep it compressed throughout and expel air as you go.

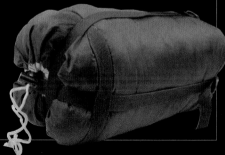

184
Keep a secret

If spilling the beans is going to lead to a whole heap of trouble, you need to be able to keep your secrets safe.

- Try to look and act calm when you have something to hide.
- When you're keeping a big secret, your body can give away what your mouth doesn't. Control your physical movements, like twitching or repeatedly scratching your nose. Maintain eye contact but don't stare.
- Imagine what might get asked of

you and then prepare your answers. If you act casually, no-one will have any reason to suspect a thing.

- Stay away from the sensitive topic if possible. If someone starts to sniff around it, don't get drawn into a series of yes and no answers. Pre-prepare a convincing, natural-seeming change of subject.
- Throw your questioner off the rails by keeping it looking as though you're remembering true events, rather than any little cover-ups you might have invented.

- Looking to the top left indicates you're scouring your memory, to the top right indicates you're using your imagination.
- If you need an alibi, make it convincing, untraceable (don't blame your oblivious best mate, who's just a phone call away) and run it through your head plenty of times before you spout it.
- If the above diversionary tactics don't keep you above suspicion, you may be forced into stretching the truth somewhat.

185
Fall off a bike safely

Whether you're on traffic-choked streets or a mountain trail, always be prepared to take a tumble.

■ You have to get over the reflex of sticking your arms out to break your fall. You'll gravel your palms at best, or break something at worst – broken wrists and collar bones are the commonest injuries when people fall of a bike.

■ On a lower-speed fall, keep your hands on the grips and let the end of the handlebar take the brunt of the fall.

■ For higher-speed falls, learn to tuck and roll: tuck your chin into your chest, pull your arms in and let your body roll through the fall on your shoulder.

■ If you fall backwards, slap your arm against the ground before your head or torso hits to defuse the energy of the fall.

■ Practise on grass, so if it happens on the road you know instinctively what to do.

■ Oh, and wear a helmet. A good one. Always.

186
Bowl a googly

What's a googly?

A leg-spin bowler normally bowls a 'leg break', which spins from the 'leg' side to the 'off' side. When the ball is released from the bowler's hand it spins anti-clockwise as it travels towards the batsman.

A googly is an occasional surprise delivery that turns the other way – from the off side towards the leg side. The batsman, thinking it's a leg break, will expect the ball to turn away from him – his confusion will often have dire consequences.

The googly turns the other way because it is released from the back of the hand, wrist cocked, ball spinning clockwise.

How do I bowl one?

Grip:
- Hold the ball in the palm with the seam parallel to the palm.
- Spread your index and middle

Grip

finger to grip the ball.
- The ring and little fingers rest against the side of the ball, the bend of the ring finger against the seam. The thumb can rest on the ball, but no pressure should be applied with it.

Practise the following slowly at first and master it before trying it at full speed:
- Run or walk up to bowl.
- As you reach the point of

release your wrist should be at 180° to the ground, the palm of your hand open upwards, and the back of your hand facing the batsman.
- As you release the ball, use the ring finger to apply most of the spin, rotating the ball clockwise towards the batsman.

Getting this right takes hours of practice and dedication.

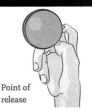

About to release

Point of release

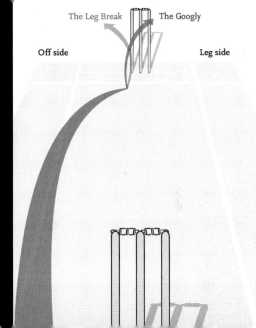

The Leg Break   The Googly

Off side   Leg side

187
Move silently through a forest

1 Stow your gear

Get rid of as much equipment as you can spare, then redistribute the rest around your body so that it doesn't knock together as you move. Wrap metal kit in cloth to muffle it. Tighten your clothing to avoid it rustling, and if possible wear boots or moccasins with soft, lightweight soles.

2 Get into rhythm

Breathe regularly through your nose and avoid holding your breath no matter how tense the situation. If in a group, try to match steps with each other – it gives off less noise (and less information to any listener). Watch where you're placing every foot and try to walk over nothing but bare earth or live foliage.

3 Tread carefully

If in a hurry, place your heel on the ground first then bring the rest of the foot down. Try to balance on the outer edge of your boots only. When backing up, walk on the ball of the foot – the area behind the toes.

Build an igloo

- Locate an area where the snow is packed hard. Begin to carve out breeze-block-sized lumps with a snow saw or snow spade.

- An igloo is built in an upward spiral. The first few blocks laid should only be a few centimetres high. The blocks slant upwards from the ground so the first circular layer gets steadily higher.

- When the first layer is finished, the last block's high end should be 30-45cm tall. You can then continue to build rectangular blocks on top of this spiral base.

- Overlap the blocks and shape them so that they lean inward (and eventually join). Cut a hole under the wall for an entrance. This will also serve as a 'sink' where cold air can escape, plus it will allow ventilation.

- Hot air from your body rises and is trapped inside the dome. It melts the roof of the igloo, forming water which refreezes to reinforce the structure. Cold air falls and flows away to the outside. In a very cold, snowy environment, an igloo will keep you warmer than a tent.

189
Mountain board

Snow all melted on your favourite ski run? Try the increasingly popular snowboarding with wheels. Learn on baby slopes with a good teacher before trying any kind of serious descent.

■ On your way up the mountain check the path that you are going to come down on. Avoid roots and big rocks which will do your board serious damage.

■ Like mounting a snowboard, position your mountain board so it can't roll down the hill. Put your feet into the footstraps and balance, bending your knees.

■ Jump up and land pointing down the mountain. The closest thing to mountain boarding is riding a bike down hill with no hands – the faster you go, the more stable you are.

■ Shift your weight using your heels and toes to turn and to slow down.

■ Unlike a snowboard, you have a handbrake, but try not to wear it out before you get to the bottom.

190
Make olive oil

These days, lots of people are growing their own fruit and veg in their gardens and green spaces – self-sufficiency is big.

But making your own olive oil? That's taking it to the next level. And it's not that hard if you are in a Mediterranean climate.

Harvest fresh olives and grind them, stone and all, into a paste, using an electric mill. Squeeze this paste or centrifuge it, and collect the resulting juice.

This is your oil, albeit mixed with the watery olive juice. Leave this liquid standing for an hour, and it will separate itself.

Siphon off the oil, bottle it and be the envy of your less knowledgeable neighbours.

191
Find out what you want to know

You don't have to be a detective or a barrister to get someone to divulge the info you need – you just have to be smart.

To successfully extract information, you need to know, a) just what it is you want to know and, b) whether or not you're asking the right person.

Do your homework before you start interrogating. If your subject has something to hide, you can either lull them into a false sense of security by pretending you're way off track, thus getting them to let their guard down, or you can hit a nerve and keep jangling it, letting them think that

resistance is futile, because you already know so much.

Keep control of the conversation. Observe give-away signs that show they could be covering up (forced smiles, sweating, rapid eye movement). Look out for answers that evade the questions without truly answering them.

Play down how important it is that they reveal their knowledge. If your subject can be convinced it's no big deal, they're less likely to cling onto it. The more you convince someone that their secret is huge, the more likely they are to bury it.

192
Survive a fall into water from a height

Your plummet into the sea is going to sting far more than your worst-ever belly-flop. How best to minimise the damage this megasplash is going to rain down on you?

1 If you have enough time, slow yourself down by spreading yourself out as much as possible – face down, arch your back, arms out and tilt your head up. More surface area equals more wind resistance equals less speed.

2 As the water gets closer, straighten up so you will be going into the impact feet first. Hold your legs tight together, arms straight above you and lean back slightly.

3 Point your toes down as you go into the water to minimise the effects of surface tension. Take a breath.

4 The air might well have been knocked out of you on entry – so get to the surface by following the direction of the bubbles your splashdown created. After all, it would be a tad annoying to drown after surviving such a fall.

193
Fold a parachute

You can't just land a parachute, unclip it and wander off. It needs to be properly packed so it will work on the next jump. You must learn the correct method from a qualified instructor.

Space and rigging
You can fold a parachute outdoors in fine weather, or indoors, but you need plenty of space. The first step is to lay out the canopy and its rigging ropes fully and make sure nothing is tangled.

Folding the canopy
Once the rigging lines are free and untangled, an instructor will teach you how to fold the canopy, step by step. First the canopy must be untangled and not caught up in the rigging. Then the instructor will show you how to fold the canopy so that it packs down small enough to fit into the chute bag. It is folded in such a way that it will open swiftly when deployed.

Coiling the rigging
With the canopy packed in the bag, it is time to coil the rigging neatly so it will unfurl swiftly and won't snag on anything. Depending on the chute design, the rigging may be stowed in the bag or held in quick release elastic loops.

That final check
You and your instructor will sign off your final efforts. But remember, your life depends on the safe functioning of that chute. If you are at all worried, get it checked by your instructor so you can jump with confidence.

Cook food in a subterranean oven

A good (and fun) way of cooking in the field is the subterranean oven.

Begin by making a normal fire. Place a lot of stones in the fire, then dig a hole more than big enough for your stones in the earth nearby. When the stones are hot enough (so hot you can't pick them up), kick them (carefully!) into the hole you just dug.

Put green leaves and branches on top of the stones, wrap your food in foil and place on top. Then cover with sand, earth and more foliage.

After an hour or two (depending on what you're cooking), unearth your grub and Bob's your uncle: oven-baked dinner.

Check it is fully cooked before you tuck in, particularly meat and fish.

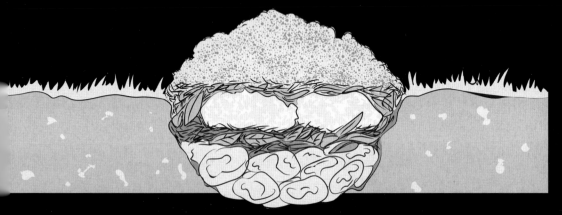

195
Create a codeword system

Keep it simple enough to remember yet very difficult for somebody to guess. A complex code is no use if you get confused yourself, and whoever is in on your scheme also needs to be fully competent in recalling it.

Avoid cliched terms like 'code blue', military speak or obscure sentences. Instead use everyday phrases and words that won't draw the attention of any eavesdroppers.

The misdirection of words is the key to building a solid codeword system. Details about time can be obscured by agreeing to add two hours or more to the timeframe you're discussing.

Coded speak occurs regularly in civilian situations. Doctors may name 'Dr Castle' or a similar fictitious person as a secret request for security when dealing with a potentially dangerous patient.

When lawyers discuss personal injury claims in front of a client, one lawyer may state to the other that the client only has 'soft tissue' injuries, a secret alert that he thinks the client is faking his injuries.

196
Improve your memory

Medical experts recommend the following general guidelines to boost your memory:

1 Stay intellectually active through learning, training or reading.

2 Keep physically active to promote blood flow to the brain.

3 Socialise, keep your sleep time regular and eat nutritiously.

When you're tired, mnemonics can prove a handy way to remember long lists. Army snipers use the mnemonic 'FLAPWIW' (pronounced 'flapwoo') as a checklist for why they may have missed their target. This stands for:

Firing position, **L**ight **A**ttachments, **P**ositional support, **W**ind, **I**nefficient zero, **W**et/oily ammunition.

Another popular mnemonic every British soldier needs is:

Teamwork, **E**nthusiasm, **S**tamina, **T**enacity, **I**nitiative, **C**ourage, **L**oyalty, **E**xcellence, **S**ense of humour.

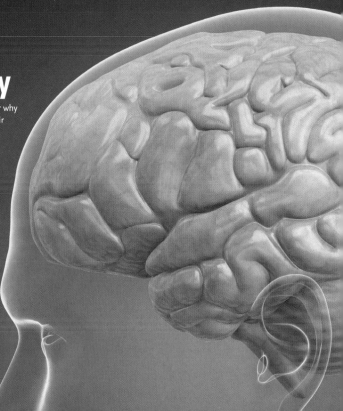

197
Purify water

To be sure natural water is fit to drink you need to purify by filtering and then boiling it, or by distilling it.

Filtering and boiling

A filter will remove the worst impurities from water. Use coffee filter papers, kitchen towels or a piece of cloth with a fine weave. Pour the water through your filter several times.

Filtering does not remove bacteria and micro-organisms. You will need to boil the water to kill them. Boiling for ten minutes kills almost everything and it is not possible to kill more by boiling longer.

Distilling

If the weather is sunny, dig a pit one-foot deep in the ground and put a container in the centre. Cover the pit with a sheet of plastic secured around the edges.

Put a stone in the centre of the plastic to weigh it down. The sun's heat will draw water out of the ground.

The water will condense on the underside of the plastic and drip into the container. This water is fit to drink.

198
Travel light

Little things add up, so don't let yourself get away with anything.

If you're aiming to travel with just a small backpack or suitcase, bulk is likely to be just as troublesome as weight, so it's vital to minimise the amount of air you're carrying around.

Iron all clothes for ultimate flatness, and take the smallest toiletries bag you can find. Most essential bathroom items are available in extra-small sizes for travellers nowadays.

Take a sealable plastic bag for storing food and drink – you'll be glad you did if something leaks.

Once you're on the road, don't stuff your dirty clothes into the nearest available corner – keep them in a separate compartment, packed as flat as possible. And don't bother picking up souvenirs – a compact digital camera will store all the memories you need.

199
Beat cramp

That sudden and often acute muscle pain most of us have at some point suffered, often when exercising, is the affected muscle shortening, or 'over contracting'.

Why? Loss of electrolytes, excessive heat, lack of fluids or nerve compression to name but four reasons. Different causes are helped in different ways, so it's best to take an overlapping approach to beating cramp rather than focusing on what you think is the single cause.

Overall, good nutrition, being properly hydrated and eating a diet with appropriate levels of sodium, magnesium, calcium and potassium will stand you in good stead against cramps.

They will still sneak through, however, and will require immediate physical attention. Stretch the specific muscles that are cramping and gently massage them to increase blood flow.

During calf and thigh cramps – two of the most common – the leg should be extended while you stretch them.

And it can't hurt (alright, it might a bit) to pinch your top lip sharply – many people claim this induces a nervous reaction that causes the cramp to disappear. If it doesn't work, at least you've distracted yourself.

Catch a fish

You don't need hi-tech kit to catch a fish – improvisation and patience will do.

Make a rod
This needs to be sturdy but with some give. Cut a living branch 2-3m long and whittle off any side branches. Tie your fishing line to the end.

Make a hook
Size isn't everything; a small hook will catch large and small fish. If you don't have proper hooks in your kit, you can improvise them (tip 145). A float fixed to the line above the hook gives you a clue where the hook is and shows when a fish strikes. Use a feather or a cork as a float.

Find some bait
Bait hides the hook and attracts the fish. Bread is a simple and effective bait, or you can use sweetcorn or berries that overhang the water. Live baits such as worms and grasshoppers continue to wriggle on the hook and are excellent for attracting fish. Throwing extra bait into the water where you are fishing can attract fish to your area. Check the stomach of the first fish you catch to see what it is feeding on.

Choose a spot
Fish retreat to deep shaded waters when it is hot and water levels are low. When the weather is cold, fish seek out shallow water warmed by the sun. They rest up in slack water on the outside of a bend or in a small tributary.

Common freshwater fish:
Roach, bream, gudgeon, carp, perch, pike, eel.

201
Paraglide

Want to soar through the air but haven't got enough time, patience or money to get your pilot's licence? Then paragliding could be just the sport for you. (Note: This really ought to go without saying, but don't try this without expert guidance and equipment!)

You will need: a paraglider wing, harness and helmet. Warm gear, gloves and strong boots.

Choose a nice day for it. Light wind and no rain is perfect. A cloudy day is better than baking sunshine.

Plan your flight. Don't just fly off into the sunset. An instructor should give you a detailed flightplan and a landing spot to aim for.

'Inflate' your wing by laying it on the hillside. Then face the wing with the wind on your back and pull on your A-risers, the lines attached to the nearest edge.

Your wing will billow up and when it's overhead, turn around facing the breeze with your steering toggles in each hand. The combination of wind and forward movement will inflate your sail and float you up.

Steer by pulling your left toggle to go left and vice versa. To slow down as you land, pull down both toggles.

In good conditions flights of 1-3 hours are common, so use the loo before you set out.

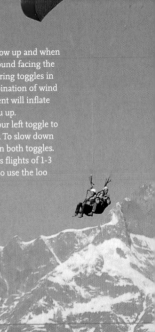

202
Make a net

Always a handy survival item to have, a net is relatively easy to make as long as you have a ball of (strong) string or a coil of fishing line. The easiest net to make is one you can cast, stretch across a stream or use to trap mammals.

- To make a 6ft x 3ft net with a one-inch mesh, cut 37 six-foot lengths of string and lay them on the floor horizontally one inch apart.
- The vertical cross strings need to be 10% longer than the depth of the net, so cut 73 40-inch strings. Lay them at one-inch intervals at right-angles across the six-foot strings so what you have laid out on the floor in front of you looks like a net.
- Then, beginning in the top left corner, move down the untied vertical strings, tying them at each intersection. And there you have it – a net.

Now find something worth catching:

- To trap fish in a stream, tie the three-foot net ends to sticks and push them into the stream bed, allowing some give in the net.
- To make a dip net, form a hoop from a wire coat hanger or a thin pine branch after threading the two ends of the net on. Tie the sides.

203
Camouflage yourself

Disguise your shape

The element of surprise is an essential skill for any soldier. Your goal is to become part of the environment and blend into the background, so take note of the colour and texture of the vegetation around you. Avoid wearing garish colours and stick to muted tones of green, brown and black. Increase your camouflage by attaching uneven clumps of grass and leaves to your clothing (belt, pockets and hat, for example) to soften the edges of your body.

Apply in moderation

Too much is as bad as too little. If you dress up like a walking bush you're going to be spotted a mile off. Overdoing it on the foliage also has a practical downside – stuffing your clothing with every leaf, twig and fern you can lay your hands on will make it difficult to move and will make you rustle as much as if you were tucking into a bag of crisps!

The sky is your enemy

Finally, stick to hedges, bushes and trees, and try to keep to the shadows. Silhouetting yourself against the sky – known in the Army as 'skylining' – is asking for trouble. Your outline will be clearly defined, making you stick out like a sore thumb. Gaps such as gateways can also silhouette you – avoid them if you can.

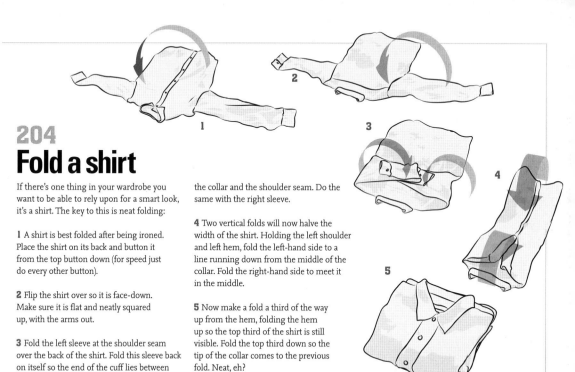

204
Fold a shirt

If there's one thing in your wardrobe you want to be able to rely upon for a smart look, it's a shirt. The key to this is neat folding:

1 A shirt is best folded after being ironed. Place the shirt on its back and button it from the top button down (for speed just do every other button).

2 Flip the shirt over so it is face-down. Make sure it is flat and neatly squared up, with the arms out.

3 Fold the left sleeve at the shoulder seam over the back of the shirt. Fold this sleeve back on itself so the end of the cuff lies between the collar and the shoulder seam. Do the same with the right sleeve.

4 Two vertical folds will now halve the width of the shirt. Holding the left shoulder and left hem, fold the left-hand side to a line running down from the middle of the collar. Fold the right-hand side to meet it in the middle.

5 Now make a fold a third of the way up from the hem, folding the hem up so the top third of the shirt is still visible. Fold the top third down so the tip of the collar comes to the previous fold. Neat, eh?

205
Exercise in the office

Deskbound life is bad for fitness. Moving a mouse doesn't count as exercise, so keep yourself ticking over with a few routines:

■ Stretching is essential to promote blood flow and prevent stiffness. Stretch your legs out regularly, and stretch your back by putting your arms out wide and leaning back, pushing back your arms. Make sure your posture is good when you are sitting in your chair.

■ Tighten your stomach muscles and hold for six seconds. Repeat six times, twice a day.

Take a small ball to work and squeeze it behind a knee 10 times, then switch knees. Lift your legs using the balls of your feet, repeating until your legs start to ache slightly.

■ Keep on the move. Moving in your seat, jigging a leg and switching your weight keeps you active. Internal email or call to make? Walk to the recipient's desk and deliver your message in person. Taking a screen break? Take a walk while you do. Rolling your wrists frequently is a good way to stave off work-related injuries.

206
Build a natural shelter

Here's a good way to build a natural shelter from materials found in any wood:

1 Gather some sticks – one bigger and longer than the others to use as the 'spine' of your new home, and some of varying lengths that will form its 'ribs'. Collect brush and foliage for the walls and floor.

2 Wedge your big spine stick firmly between two trees. Now rest the medium-sized sticks against the spine to form a triangular shelter.

3 Cover the floor inside with the brush – the bare earth would sap your heat so you need to raise yourself above it. Festoon the outside with foliage, held in place with more sticks, to provide further protection and insulation.

4 Build a fire outside your shelter. Rest well.

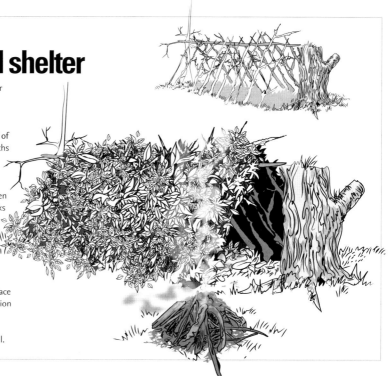

207
Do a cartwheel

It's a good idea to try this on a padded carpet or a mattress so you don't hurt yourself. You should also learn how to do a basic handstand before attempting a cartwheel. Once mastered, though, doing cartwheels gives a good upper-body workout and develops a keen sense of balance.

1 Make sure you have plenty of space around you. Stretch both arms above your head. Point your right foot forward while turning the left slightly outwards for balance.

2 Now look forward to the point where you will place your hands. Lunge forward, keeping your back straight. Put your right hand on the floor with your fingers facing forward.

3 Rotate your left leg upwards and place your left hand on the ground, a shoulder-width apart from your right hand. Push off with your right leg.

4 Your momentum should now carry you through. Pick up your right hand as the left foot hits the floor. Continue to rotate, lifting your left hand as the right foot hits the floor.

5 Finish by standing bolt upright with your hands above your head. Grinning.

208
Toss a pancake

The proper technique starts with having the right kitchenware. A good quality non-stick frying pan makes tossing much easier.

When the pancake is almost ready, gently shake the pan to make sure it hasn't stuck. Take the pan off the heat and move it away from your body. Dip the frying pan slightly before flicking your wrist upwards. This will flip the pancake up and back towards you.

As the pancake lifts off the pan, level the frying pan and move it to catch the pancake, which should fall back the other way up.

209
Stop yourself from sneezing

Sneezing fires air out of your lungs at speeds of up to 100mph. It's an essential bodily function which removes infectious microscopic droplets. However, at times when sneezing is a social no-no, here's what you should do:

- When you first feel the tickling sensation of a sneeze coming on, press your tongue hard where the roof of your mouth meets your two front teeth. Keep pushing until the tickling sensation eases.

- Alternatively, tickle the roof of your mouth with your tongue. After a few seconds, the urge to sneeze should subside.

- Tickle your earlobe. You'll look like you are deep in thought, but in a few moments the need to sneeze should disappear.

- Don't grab your nose and hold it tight. Sneezes are commonplace events but are surprisingly violent. You could damage the blood vessels in your head. Using this technique repeatedly could even harm your hearing. Contrary to playground lore, however, your head will not explode.

BE THE BEST...

"IF CAUGHT UP IN AN AVALANCHE, TRY TO 'SWIM' WITH THE FLOW – IMAGINE BODYSURFING WITH THE TIDE"

Survive an avalanche

Despite 200 avalanche fatalities a year, statistically you're unlikely ever to encounter the white wall of death. If you are unlucky and do, though, these measures will improve your chances of survival:

1 Get moving

The number-one cause of an avalanche is… you. If you feel slippage starting under your feet, a swift jump up-slope might get you out of the danger zone. More likely, you'll see the avalanche bearing down on you. Don't hesitate – run or ski sideways as quickly as possible to get away from the centre of the fall, as this is where the greatest volume of snow is and where it's moving the fastest. If you can't get out of the way, a boulder or outcrop can provide vital shelter.

2 Start swimming

If caught up in the avalanche, try to 'swim' with the flow – imagine bodysurfing with the tide. This should keep you on or near the surface. Don't hang on to any of your gear: ski poles and packs will only snag on debris and drag you deeper. If you feel the avalanche slowing, fight to keep near the surface of the snow and fill your lungs, because the pressure's about to increase.

3 Dig or sit tight?

Even if you've survived the avalanche, you still need to be careful. Only fight your way to the surface if it's obvious you're lightly buried, as you'll burn up oxygen at a frightening rate. Otherwise, hollow out an air pocket while the snow is still loose, as it will quickly start to compact. Calm yourself for a minute and, if disorientated, work out which way is up: spit and see where it goes. Decide whether to attempt to dig your way out – the darker it is, the less likely you'll make it. If you can hear people, shout for help. Then you'll have to wait it out, conserving your air as best you can.

211
Do the perfect triceps dip

Method:

- Find something sturdy and about 30-40cm off the floor that will comfortably support your body weight (eg an exercise bench).
- Face away from the bench and take your weight on your braced arms. Your legs should be straight, resting on your heels.

- Lower your body by bending your arms.
- When your arms reach a 90° angle, hold your position for a second.
- Push back up with your arms until they are straight.
- Lower yourself again to begin your next dip.

Tips:

- You should keep your back straight throughout the movement.
- Exhale as you lower your body downwards and inhale as you rise. Do not hold your breath.
- Concentrate on good technique rather than

speed – you will get much more benefit.
- Try to progressively increase the number of dips you can do in a row each time you exercise.

Muscle group worked:
Upper arms

Step 1

Step 2

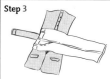

Step 3

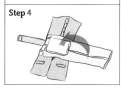

Step 4

212
Pack a suitcase

- 'Bundle wrapping' not only crams the most clothing into the least space, it requires no folding so produces no creases, and stretches your clothing to help eliminate wrinkles.
- Layer your clothing in the following order: jackets, shirts, trousers, knitwear. Ensure each is laid out smoothly.
- Place the 'core' item on top. This should be a bag about the size of an A3 piece of paper, stuffed with soft items like underwear.

The collars of your bottom items should poke out from the sides.
- Firmly wrap each item, one at a time, around the core. When down to the shirts, wrap each arm in an 'X' configuration.
- Use your suitcase's internal straps to hold the final bundle tight enough so it doesn't break free.
- Stuff shoes with socks to keep their shape.
- On arrival, unfold the pieces and allow them to relax before hanging. Smooth job!

Step 5

Step 6

Step 7

Step 8

213
Patrol in formation

Arrowhead

When soldiers use it: When patrolling open spaces, usually in daytime.

Benefits: Every soldier is facing forwards so will be able to counter any attack.

How they do it: This patrol gets its name from its 'V' shape (pictured). With one person at the front, the rest of the group is split into pairs and staggered behind, and to the side of, the lead person. The spacing depends on what the ground and vegetation is like, but would be a maximum of 20 metres, or much less in poor visibility.

Extended line

When soldiers use it: During an attack or flushing enemy soldiers out of a forest.

Benefits: Soldiers can cover (and search) a large area.

How they do it: Soldiers spread out in a line at even intervals. They then move forward as one, searching the ground as they go. It is highly effective but calls for extreme concentration, particularly in wooded areas, because it is vital that each person can always see the men nearest to them.

Single file

When soldiers use it: If they want to cover ground quickly as a group.

Benefits: It's an easy formation to control and is good for quick communication.

How they do it: Soldiers only use this formation at night because it makes them very visible. One person leads the way while the rest of the group follows in his or her footsteps. Perfect for travelling in an alleyway or along a river bed.

Wash with one pint of water

If water is scarce, it's still important to keep yourself clean as often as possible to avoid infection. A pint is enough to do this.

Use the first two mouthfuls to brush your teeth. Fungal infections will quickly affect parts of the body that make contact with each other, so next clean your armpits, groin area and between your toes.

These are the areas you should wash first – the rest of you can get by for a few days without too much trouble.

If you're sparing with the water, wash other parts of your body, starting with your face. You may even be able to save some for a shave.

215
Clean a kettle

Limescale deposits build up inside your kettle and before long your morning cuppa won't taste quite as good as it should. So clean your kettle regularly.

You will need: Water, white vinegar or lemon juice, a brush (optional)

1 Fill the kettle halfway with water.
2 Fill the remaining half with white vinegar or add 30ml of lemon juice.
3 Boil the resulting mixture.
4 Leave it for a few hours or overnight.
5 Pour it all out.
6 Fill it again, this time full of water.
7 Boil again.
8 Repeat steps 6 and 7 until you can no longer smell the vinegar or lemon juice.
9 Reward yourself with a nice brew.

216
Hoist a flag

Modern flagpoles consist of a mast and a continuous loop of rope – the halyard. Attached to the halyard are two toggles or clips – one to snap onto the top of the flag, one for the bottom. The important thing to ensure is that the halyard loop has been created by a rope being knotted together – don't use the flag itself to complete the loop, as this will put strain on the flag material. It's the halyard that needs to take the strain. Pull down on the halyard to raise your flag.

217
Score a basket

Here's how to score with a 'set shot' – the bread-and-butter basketball shot, which you'd use for a free throw:

- Hold the ball with your shooting hand on the back and the other on the side, both palms spread.
- Concentrate on the basket. You're aiming to drop straight through the hoop, not come off the backboard.
- Bend your knees, feet shoulder-width apart.
- Extend your knees and

arms at the same time to jump and throw. (You rarely throw with your feet on the ground.)

- As you rise from the knees, push the ball up with your shooting hand as the other hand supports. Keep your throwing arm in line with the basket, not straying off to either side.
- Release the ball just as your arm fully extends.
- As you release the ball flick your wrist. Your middle and index fingers should

be the last ones touching the ball.

- Let your shooting hand follow through in line with the basket, as if guiding it in.
- Practise as much as you can, shooting from different angles and distances

- Mastered the set shot? To score a slam dunk (pictured), launch yourself above the basket and slam the ball down through it. Easy.

218
Learn a language

The Army's Intelligence Corps has its own linguists who speak and translate many languages. Here are the secrets to learning another lingo.

Little and often

The key to learning a language is to do a little often. Spend 20-30 minutes learning new words or phrases, then take a break. Test yourself later.

Learning aids

The best way to learn a language is to work with a tutor who is a native speaker.

If you need to work on your own there are books, cassettes, CDs and videos to help you. If you want to speak a language, then recordings are a big help.

You can load these on to an iPod and learn a few words in your spare time. Find someone you can practice with, preferably a native speaker.

Reading and writing

A new language has to be built up, step by step, as you learn pronouns, simple verbs, different tenses, nouns, genders, rules of grammar and so on. It can seem daunting at first, so set yourself targets and work steadily using a 'teach yourself' course.

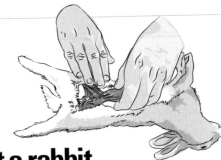

219
Gut a rabbit

To minimise bleeding, let your (humanely and legally killed) rabbit cool before gutting – but don't leave it so long that it starts to go off. Use your bare hands to do the gutting wherever possible, as knife punctures can lead to contaminated meat.

1 Using a sharp-tipped knife make a small, shallow incision just below the rabbit's ribs. Then insert two fingers and pull the belly fully open.

2 Holding the rabbit by the chest and back legs, swing it downwards in one quick motion so the entrails drop out.

3 Pull the entrails clear at the back end, then carefully grip the stomach to pull them away at the front end.

4 Pierce the diaphragm with your knife then pull out the heart and lungs. There you are – one rabbit ready for cooking.

Walk a tightrope

Only do this with a rope that's close to the ground – don't try what you see in the picture! Footwear should have a thin, flexible sole (like school plimsolls or ballet shoes). Alternatively, go barefoot – then you can grip the rope between the big and second toes.

Step forward with one foot onto the rope. Gradually shift the weight forward onto this foot. Extend your arms to either side to help with balance. Stare straight ahead, never downwards, and concentrate on balancing your weight on this foot.

Once steady, smoothly bring the trailing foot forward and place it in front of the first. Continue steadily, only moving the trailing foot forward when you are ready.

221
Run

Jogging is one of the cornerstones of fitness. Get your technique right first and you're on the road to stamina, strength and good health.

- The key is moving smoothly and efficiently without wasting energy or putting excess strain on any part of your body.
- Find a steady pace and rhythm you can keep up, don't go flat out.
- Breathe long and deep, in through the nose and out through the mouth. Breathing in time with your footfall can help create rhythm.
- Keep your head up and your eyes looking forward.
- Keep your shoulders drawn back – don't hunch over. Push your hips forward as you run.
- Move your arms in rhythm with your running – swing each arm in time with the opposite leg. But don't move your arms excessively; keep your elbows into your sides and avoid rolling your shoulders.
- Make sure your knees and feet are moving in line so that movement is concentrated forward, not up and down or side to side.
- Strike the surface of the ground with your heel first, then roll off with the ball of your feet.

Pass an interview

Every soldier and officer in the Army must pass an interview, as well as physical and mental tests, before they can join. You too are certain to need to pass interviews during your life.

- Interviewers respond to positive physical signs in the candidate. These are: good posture, firm handshake and a smile. Get them right from the word go.
- Interviewers also look for signs of professionalism. These are: punctuality, presentability, politeness, and appropriate behaviour.
- As Sun Tzu said, a battle is won before it is ever fought. What goes for war goes for any challenge such as an interview – preparation is everything.
- Work out what the interviewer wants before you get to the interview. Research the company, its products, its history and who will be interviewing you. Interviewers are impressed by forethought.
- Prepare for those tricky questions, like 'What are your weak points?' That's a tough question requiring a well-rehearsed answer. And be ready for the surprise question such as 'What book are you reading?' or something topical.
- Be relaxed, confident, positive, enthusiastic – and genuine.

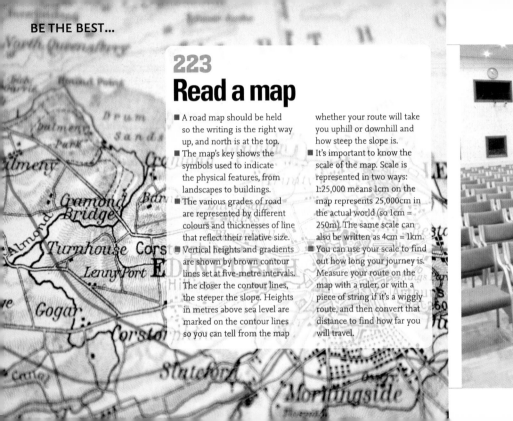

223
Read a map

- A road map should be held so the writing is the right way up, and north is at the top.
- The map's key shows the symbols used to indicate the physical features, from landscapes to buildings.
- The various grades of road are represented by different colours and thicknesses of line that reflect their relative size.
- Vertical heights and gradients are shown by brown contour lines set at five-metre intervals. The closer the contour lines, the steeper the slope. Heights in metres above sea level are marked on the contour lines so you can tell from the map whether your route will take you uphill or downhill and how steep the slope is.
- It's important to know the scale of the map. Scale is represented in two ways: 1:25,000 means 1cm on the map represents 25,000cm in the actual world (so 1cm = 250m). The same scale can also be written as 4cm = 1km.
- You can use your scale to find out how long your journey is. Measure your route on the map with a ruler, or with a piece of string if it's a wiggly route, and then convert that distance to find how far you will travel.

224
Speak in public

For many, it's the stuff of nightmares – speaking to a packed auditorium, presenting to a round table of colleagues or thanking a marquee of friends and family for coming to your wedding.

But public speaking is something you can learn, it doesn't have to come naturally at first. It's all about building your confidence and learning a few tricks.

Practice will get you some of the way to combating those nerves.

Stand alone and rehearse out loud how you would ideally deliver your speech. Imagine a crowd lapping it up just the way you'd like them to. Try it out in different ways, at different speeds and with different intonations. Get used to projecting your voice and speaking clearly.

Draft your speech so that there's no lag. Start out on topic and stay there. When it comes to saying it in front of an audience, nothing will put you off more than seeing their attention drift.

Once you're on the spot, calmly focus on the message you're there to get across. Don't be distracted by your audience. Pace yourself, allow pauses for effect, feel free to gesture when you really want to make a point. Above all, enunciate clearly and keep your breathing steady.

Be confident – after all, if you know you're going to deliver a belter of a speech, what have you got to be nervous about?

225
Build a barbecue

You will need: Bricks, stones, a metal grille, charcoal briquettes, dry firewood, skewers

- Find a flat piece of ground and lay out your metal grille (if you use the one out of your oven, give it a good wash afterwards).
- Use skewers instead of a grille for barbecued kebabs (pictured).
- Build your bricks from the ground up, based around the size of the grille, so that you have a pit about two feet high that it can rest on top of.
- Lay stones and pebbles at the bottom of the pit to prevent scorched earth. If you have bricks to spare, two layers will

form a good fireproof base.
- Lay your firewood on top of the stones. If you have lighter fuel, squirt some over the wood before lighting. If you don't, lay paper (or cardboard egg boxes) beneath the wood and light that first. When the wood is

alight, add the briquettes.
- Let your fire burn for at least 20 minutes until the flames have died down and the coals are turning grey and white. It will now be kicking out intense heat.
- Start cooking your food on the grille. Think veggie as well as

meat and fish. Make sure it is all fresh and fully defrosted.
- Different foods cook at different speeds; the hottest part of the grille is the centre, use the sides for slower cooking.
- Make sure all food is fully cooked before serving. Tuck in.

WARNING

RIP CURRENTS
You could be swept out
and drown
IF IN DOUBT, DON'T GO OUT.

226
Survive a rip current

Rip currents occur when sea water heads back out to sea from the shore. They are particularly dangerous for weak swimmers.

If caught in a current, never try to fight it as you'll just exhaust yourself in the process. Instead, try to swim parallel to the shoreline and when you feel the force lessen, swim away from the current toward the shore.

If you're unable to swim out of the current, calmly tread water (tip 47) and draw attention to yourself by waving one arm and yelling for help.

BE THE BEST...

227
Bow

Here's how men should bow to a member of the Royal Family:

- Stand to attention with your arms at your sides.
- Bow by bending from the neck or shoulders. (Don't bow from the waist.)
- At the same time, briefly lower your eyes.
- Bow again when the Royal leaves.

228
Pass your driving test

One of the first qualifications you get in the Army is your driving licence. Here's how to pass that nerve-wracking test:

- Take plenty of lessons with a good instructor – and 'good' does not mean 'nice'. A teacher who pulls you up on every mistake is better than a kindly soul who's afraid to hurt your feelings.
- Get as much practice as possible between lessons, and don't insist on taking the test before the instructor thinks you're ready. Pick a test time when you're not going to be stressed about other things such as exams.
- Don't get wound up – the main reason behind most driving test failures is nothing more than anxiety. You have to stay calm and remember that you can still pass even if you get a few small things wrong. In fact, you're allowed to make up to 15 minor mistakes before the examiner is obliged to fail you. One major error, however, and you will be failed.
- Turn up in good time with your theory test certificate and both parts of your provisional licence. Make sure the car you're going to take the test in has an up-to-date road tax disc, MOT and insurance.
- Don't let yourself become flustered if you get confused by the examiner's directions. You will not fail your test for missing a turn-off.

Step 1

Step 2

Step 3

Step 4

Step 5

229
Throw

1 Stand sideways on from your target with your feet slightly wider than shoulder-width apart. Fix your eyes on the target.

2 Bring your throwing arm back behind your head. Your elbow should be at shoulder height and cocked at 90°, forearm perpendicular to the ground. Your throwing hand should be

level with the top of your head. Your other arm should be pointing towards the target.

3 Twist your upper body towards your target and hurl your arm forward as your weight shifts, snapping your arm and wrist towards the target. Your non-throwing arm should travel in the opposite direction to

your throwing arm, balancing it out.

4 Release your projectile when your throwing arm is almost fully extended. Your throwing arm must follow through towards the target.

5 Your momentum will carry you forward onto your front leg – bend that knee.

230
Get rid of cockroaches

Cockroaches love nothing better than an untidy house, so if you discover their presence the first thing to do is clean up. Store food in containers or secure cupboards and clean up any crumbs.

Wipe all work surfaces with disinfectant and check behind utility units – they love the dark. Also check for leaking plumbing, as they often congregate around water sources.

Make your own insecticide by mixing equal measures of baking soda and powdered sugar and leaving it out on a dish – the baking soda element proves fatal to them. Cockroaches also hate bay leaves.

The thing they hate most is a professional pest controller. Get one in.

231
Survive a flood

When flood waters hit, you don't always have time to run. A flash flood can turn a peaceful street into a flowing river in a matter of minutes, in which time your conventional methods of escape may be cut off.

1 Be prepared

If you live in a low-lying area near a body of water, you'll need to keep the following in a safe, above-water-level location: bottled water, tinned food, warm and waterproof clothes. Look into getting flood defences installed around your property – just an inch of water can ruin a living room's worth of belongings.

2 Be fast

If it's a slow-building flood, you have time to unplug your electrical equipment, turn the electricity and gas off, and pick and choose what supplies you're going to take to high ground. Seal important documents in a plastic bag. If it's a flash flood, you may just have minutes before your home is awash.

What if you're out and about when a flash flood strikes? Travel away from the direction that the water is coming from and aim to get up high. Don't ever consider driving through flood waters – 50 per cent of deaths during floods occur when people drown after trying to drive through them.

3 Be aware

If you have access to a radio or TV, check for emergency information in your area. If you know your local geography, you should know which areas are higher up and less likely to be submerged. If you have any reason to believe that the area you live in is at risk, a little forethought could keep you and your possessions safe and dry.

232
Never be late again

Punctuality is a sign of respect. If you're continually late – be it for meetings, meals, or work – it shows a disregard for those who bother to show up on time. You can't always blame the traffic – if you have a problem, you need to take action to remedy it.

■ To be punctual you must become more aware of time itself. Always wear a watch. Make sure you have clocks in all rooms of your house and workplace. Ensure your mobile has a clock on the home screen.

■ Plan ahead. If you have an appointment, give yourself time to get to it, allowing for all the potential delays that could arise. As an experiment, try to be early for everything – you never know, it might get you there on time.

■ Re-evaluate your habits and the length of time it takes you to do them. Maybe you spend longer brushing your teeth or finding the right playlist on your iPod than you thought. Keep your belongings organised, so you're not scrabbling around for your wallet when you should have been out of the door 20 minutes ago.

233
Juggle a football

Ball-juggling, or 'keepy-uppy', isn't just for showing off. It's great to develop your touch and ball control. Here's how to learn:

Method:
- Drop the ball from about waist height onto your strongest foot.
- Volley the ball back up into your hands, making contact with the laces of your boot.
- Control the weight of the volley – not too hard or weak.
- Once you've mastered this, instead of catching the ball let it drop down to your feet again and volley it back up a second time before you catch it.
- Build up progressively in this way until you can regularly do five consecutive controlled volleys followed by a catch.
- Now forget about catching the ball – just try to do as many volleys as you can each time. Try to set a new record every practice session.
- As you improve, begin to use your weaker foot, thighs and head.

Tips:
- A slightly flat ball will allow you more control while you learn.
- Hold your arms out to the sides to help your balance.
- Keep your eye on the ball.
- Keep on your toes because you'll need to move.
- Practise like mad.

234
Dowse for water

The science of dowsing – sensing and discovering an underground water source – is hazy at best, but the results are often impressive. And the most important piece of equipment when hunting for hidden water supplies is your own body. Dowsing rods are only there to pick up the signals coming down your arms.

For that reason, hi-tech rods are not required – a couple of metal coat-hangers bent into L-shapes will do the job. Hold them in front of you with the longer part of each rod pointing forwards, and keep your grip fairly loose. Now walk forwards slowly and steadily.

Before you head off into the desert, you can test your dowsing powers by walking over an area where you know there is water below (a drainpipe, for example). As you reach the watery spot, the parallel metal rods should hopefully swing inwards and cross.

235
Repair a scratch on car bodywork

Army vehicles have more to worry about than imperfections in the paintwork. But repairing a scratch in the family motor can cost a packet – when in fact scratches on your car can easily be fixed yourself with the aid of some touch-up spray paint.

■ First, wipe the scratch with a mild detergent and use sandpaper to sand away any metal residue or rust that may have formed.

■ Make a stencil – get some paper and trace the scratch. Cut a hole in the paper the shape and size of the scratch.

■ Tape the paper down over the area and apply your paint to the exposed scratch.

■ Remove the stencil and leave the paint to dry for 24 hours.

■ Polish over for a nice finish.

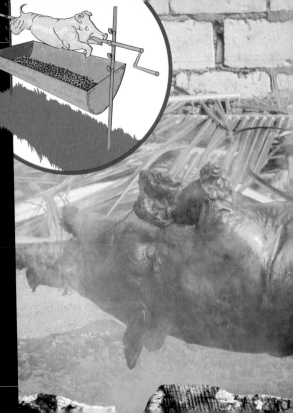

236
Spit roast a hog

1 Fill your fire pit with charcoal (the best fuel). You will need lots of it – enough for the full cooking time, including refills.

2 Position more charcoal below where the hog's shoulders and legs (the thickest parts) will be. Wait until the coals are glowing red before cooking (build up to a heat of about 180°C).

3 Select a young, well-fed pig of about 20kg (to feed 40 people). Prepare and season it, and skewer it on the spit lengthways (through anus and mouth), with the spit as close as possible to the pig's central axis.

4 Place the spitted pig on the supports one to two feet above the heat (depending on its size) – close enough to cook the inside without burning the outside.

5 The bigger the beast, the longer it takes to cook – allow 4-6 hours for a 20kg pig. Rotate the pig regularly on the spit for even roasting. Baste regularly with cooking oil and juices that have collected in a drip tray, to keep the meat moist and tasty.

6 The beast is done when a cooking thermometer shows the internal temperature at the meat's thickest part is 80°C.

7 Let it rest off the heat for 30 minutes before carving.

237
Tie a Windsor knot

The Windsor knot will smarten up any shirt and tie combination, but is best suited to shirts with a spread collar. Here's how it's tied:

1 Start with the wide end of the tie about 30cm below the narrow end. Pass the wide end over the narrow end.

2 Bring the wide end up between your collar and your tie.

3 Pass it over the tie and back down. Loop the wide end underneath the narrow end, so the wide end is facing off to the left and is inside out.

4 Bring the wide end across the front from left to right.

5 Pull it up between your collar and the tie.

6 Now bring the wide end down through the knot in front. Tighten the knot carefully using both hands and pull it up to the collar.

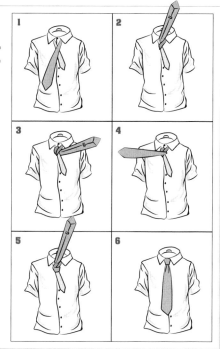

238
Tie a turban

Traditional Sikh headwear, the turban (or Dastar) is a spiritually significant item of clothing. Sikh soldiers wear one instead of a beret. There's a knack to putting one on.

1 Begin by folding the turban in half, then in half again until you have a scarf-like length of cloth. Make a small fold along one edge (about an inch) to neaten it up.

2 Place one end of the turban at the back of your head, and pin it with your finger to the back of your neck. Bring the turban round your head from right to left, so it comes around just above your left eyebrow and round the back again, so it folds over the end. Keep it tight at all times, and then bring it around again so it's now wrapped twice around your head.

3 As you bring it around a third time, start lower on the right-hand side and wrap upwards as you reach the left side of your head, evening out its distribution. Keep straightening out the cloth as you wrap, firming out any creases. Wrap symmetrically until you have the last couple of inches, which can be tucked in at the back.

4 Finally, the original end that was pinned to your neck can be pulled out through the hole in the middle, spread out and used to cover the whole top of your head, folding it back underneath the sides so it doesn't come unstuck.

239
Throw people off your trail

If they don't know you're there
You want to make sure you don't leave a trace. Don't light a fire as the smoke will let them home in on you, so if you must have one for cooking, build it at a distance from your hide. If you make camp, make sure you hide or destroy all trace of it – clear away all litter. If you had a fire, douse it completely and hide the ashes.

If they're looking for you
You need to put as much distance as you can between yourself and the pursuer. If you have the time, create a false trail, which may be as simple as running one way, retracing your steps, then running in another. The false trail could buy you valuable time.

Avoid open areas and stay out of the line of sight. If you need to rest and hide, ensure you've got more than one escape route lined up, and have a vantage point where you can see your pursuer. Make sure that not just you but also your shadow is hidden.

If they're near, throwing items into other areas may distract them or send them down the wrong trail. And you'll need to lose your smell (tip 04) so they don't sniff you out.

When choosing an area to hide, think BLISS:

B Blend in with surroundings
L Low in silhouette
I Irregular in shape
S Small in size
S Secluded

240
Do the perfect dorsal raise

Method:

- Lie face down on the ground (ideally on an exercise mat) with your legs straight and your arms clasped behind your bottom.
- Using your back muscles, raise your chest, shoulders and head off the floor.
- When you have raised your shoulders by about 6-8 inches, hold your position for two or three seconds.
- Lower yourself back to floor level in a controlled fashion (don't just drop on your nose!).
- Raise your upper body to begin your next dorsal raise.

Tips:

- Keep your hips and stomach in contact with the floor.
- Don't crane your neck upwards unnaturally.
- Breathe in as you raise your body and out as you lower it. Don't hold your breath.
- Concentrate on good technique rather than speed.
- Try to progressively increase the number of dorsal raises you can do in a row each time you exercise.

Muscle groups worked:
Lower back, stomach

Paint a room

1 Clean all surfaces with detergent and water and leave them plenty of time to dry. Surfaces that haven't been painted before should first be sanded down and given a coat of primer.

2 Cover the floor with newspaper or dust sheets. You WILL drop the occasional blob.

3 Attach low-stick masking tape to skirting boards and window frames so the paint goes to the edge of the wall but everything beyond that is protected with tape; when all is finished, you can then peel away the masking tape to reveal a neat paint line.

4 Turn the power off and unscrew plug sockets and light switches to hang clear of the wall.

5 Invest in good-quality paint, rollers and brushes. Poor-quality paint can make it hard to get an even, long-lasting finish. Cheap rollers drip everywhere and cheap brushes shed bristles.

6 Fill in your edges and corners with a small brush first – that way if you do leave brush marks, the roller will cover most of them up.

7 Load your roller with paint (not too much) and take your time to apply it in vertical strokes with even, light pressure. Never stop for lunch halfway across a wall. And if the tin says you need two coats, believe it.

8 Keep the room well ventilated while you paint – and don't let it get too hot or too cold, as this can also affect the finish.

242
Make your phone battery last longer

Getting help is the one thing most likely to save you in lots of situations. That makes mobile phones a great survival tool... but not without a battery. Here's how to keep yours alive:

1 Make your calls count – they batter the battery.
2 Set the volume low and select a short, simple ring tone (careful with 'silent' mode though – you don't want to miss a vital call).
3 Turn off vibrate mode, Bluetooth and 3G.
4 Set your screensaver to show a blank screen. Dim the display.
5 Switch it off when you're on the move.
6 Know how long does your phone battery lasts. Guess conservatively if you don't know the spec – you might need to ration out the time.
7 If power is really low, turn it off until you really need it.

243
Read the opposite sex

The other half of the species can often seem pretty inscrutable, but there are tell-tale signs that can be picked up on to let you know what they're thinking.

If you're talking to someone who keeps playing with their hair or drawing your attention to their finer assets, chances are they're flirting.

If they're directing the position of their body toward you, and aren't worried about invading your personal space, they're definitely comfortable around you.

If their body looks like they're doing whatever it takes to get away from you, chances are that's what they want to do.

Eye contact is another important factor. If they maintain it, or at least stare at your mouth while you're talking, this shows they have an interest in what you're saying.

If they seem distracted, chances are you're not of that much interest and they're looking for an escape route.

Look to see if they mimic any of your movements – this is a sure-fire sign that you have their attention.

Physical acts such as arm crossing (defiant), lip biting (anxious) or hands in pockets (relaxed in your company) are also clear signs worth paying attention to.

If your jokes are getting a lot of laughs, throw in a stinker to see if they're laughing at anything you say.

Hello	How are you? A	How are you? B	Sorry	Please
	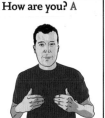			

244
Use sign language

Signing takes a long time to master, but a few basic phrases will get you started. And even if you never learn another word, just making the effort to say 'Hello' will always be appreciated.

Mouth the word at the same time as you sign it – lip-reading is an essential part of communication for many deaf people. And be warned that different countries have their own sign languages – so an American might struggle to follow your British gestures.

■ **'Hello'**
With your right forearm perpendicular to the floor, make a single outward wave of the open right hand.

■ **'How are you?'**
Touch your chest with the fingertips of both hands (pic A) then move hands forward with fists closed (pic B).

■ **'Sorry'**
Draw a circle on your chest with your closed right fist.

■ **'Please'**
Touch your chin with the fingertips of your right hand then move the hand forwards and down. 'Thank you' is just the same – the difference is in the lips.

245
Cause a scene

If you're ever looking to escape a situation, your best bet is to create a distraction. Causing a commotion is obviously pretty simple but the key to escape is not to attract attention to yourself. Starting a food fight in a café, for instance, will only draw eyes upon you as the ringleader, so use stealth.

Spread rumours, plant an object that will be found later, alter part of your environment without others seeing or persuade others to do your work for you – it's about using techniques that won't shine the spotlight on you. Whatever you try, don't risk anything dangerous or illegal – you're only endangering yourself this way.

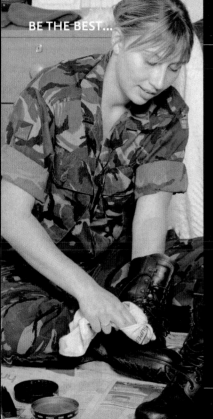

246
Polish boots

What you'll need:
Some old newspaper, two boot brushes (one marked 'on' for applying polish, one marked 'off' for removing it – keep them separate), a clean soft cloth, and an old toothbrush.

1 Prepare
Before you even open the polish, make sure you cover your carpet or floor with old newspaper. Remove the laces from your shoes so you can get to those hard-to-reach areas. Wash footwear with warm, clean water if required, and leave to dry. Brush over with the 'off' brush to remove any dust or dried dirt.

2 Polish on
Dab the bristles of the 'on' brush into the polish and rub over the footwear until polish is evenly spread over the whole upper. You may need the old toothbrush to get into all the nooks and crannies between any stitching.

Take care not to get polish on the sole.

3 Polish off
Put the boots aside for 10 minutes to allow the polish to sink in. Then, using the 'off' brush, brush rigorously with a back-and-forth motion, buffing each shoe to bring up the shine and remove any excess polish.

4 Perfect
Then dampen the clean cloth and wrap a corner of it around the first two fingers of one hand (holding the rest of the cloth tight in your palm). Dab the cloth into the polish and apply a small amount to the toe of one shoe. Gently work your way all the way round to the heal, rubbing the polish in a circular motion – this is known in the Army as 'bulling'. Again, make sure you pay particular attention to the areas between any stitching. Keep the cloth damp and re-apply polish as required.

247
Pick head lice

Monkeys pick them out and eat them. You might not want to go quite that far, but you should keep your head pest-free.

- Head lice and their eggs (nits) can affect anyone. They are easiest to remove if you have short hair.
- Soak your hair in conditioner or vegetable oil. Using a fine-toothed nit comb, comb one section of your hair several times, passing close to the scalp. Dip the comb in soapy water and remove debris from it with a tissue. Make sure the comb is clean before combing again.
- Work steadily across the scalp. Shampoo the hair thoroughly to remove the oil. Comb the dry hair and check for any surviving lice.
- Repeat this treatment if the problem persists, washing bedding and clothes at 60°C to get rid of any lingering eggs or lice.

248
Find your way without a compass

If you find yourself lost at night without a compass, the stars can be your guide.

In the northern hemisphere, if you locate Polaris, the North Star, then you've found north.

Walking towards that will take you north, away from it south.

First locate The Plough (aka the Saucepan or Big Dipper). Draw an imaginary straight line upwards from the two stars at the front of the saucepan. About five times the distance between the two stars you are drawing your line from you will find the bright star Polaris. That's north.

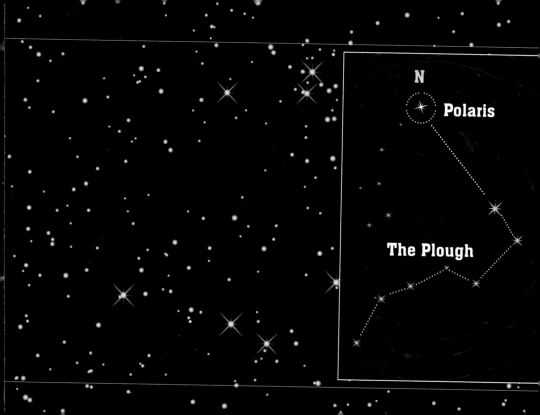

249
Fend off a
dog attack

Show no fear
A jittery target will be sized up as lunch.
Don't stare the dog in the eye or smile
(baring teeth is a sign of aggression), and
never run – your heels are an easy target.

Wait it out
Dogs get bored quickly. If you stand your
ground in a non-aggressive fashion, chances
are your opposing pooch will leave you be.

Under attack
If violently attacked, you should move to the
nearest area (dragging the dog if necessary)
where you can shield your body from attack,
like behind a door. Fight back with hard
blows to the nose, stunning the dog into
retreat. Use a weapon (eg: a stick) if you can.

250
Curtsy

Here's how females should curtsy to members of the Royal Family:

- To make a curtsy, briefly bend the knees with one foot forward.

- Create a distinct 'bobbing' movement, keeping the upper body straight.

- This should again be performed when the member of the Royal Family leaves.

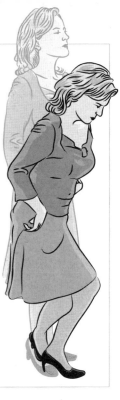

251
Build a boat

At its simplest a boat is anything that will transport you on water – a basic raft is most often your best option. Here is a sturdy raft-building method, but it requires the right equipment – in the field you'll have to improvise, depending on what materials you have to hand.

- Make the deck from planks or a board. Marine plywood is ideal, varnished to be waterproof.
- For flotation use four large (55-gallon if possible) empty metal or plastic drums. Lengths of sealed 6in plastic drainpipe can be used instead but are less buoyant.

- Bolt two lengths of 2x4in timber under the front of the deck and two more at the back.
- Place two barrels on one side, two on the other. Lash each one to the 2x4 timber using wire or strong rope. To prevent the barrels slipping you might glue metal brackets to the barrels and run the wire through them.
- A sail will be more trouble than it's worth, so fashion two simple oars from sturdy poles screwed to plywood blades. The blades can be shaped with a saw.

252
Search your house for intruders

If you return home to an open front door, or if you wake and suspect that an intruder is in your house, it's best to play safe.

Call 999 and tell the police that you suspect someone's in your house. Sit tight, and wait for the cavalry to arrive.

If you're outside, stay outside. Don't block the intruder's escape route or do anything to provoke a confrontation. If and when you see the intruder, make a mental note of their clothing and appearance so you can give the police a thorough description later. Watch to see which direction they head in when they leave.

If you're inside, call out as if speaking to a family member. This could be enough to get a burglar to make a run for it.

If you do decide to search the house, be very cautious. Make as little noise as possible moving slowly from one room to another, floor by floor.

If you do find an intruder, try to avoid a physical confrontation. They may look small, but could still be carrying a knife. Better to take in their appearance, then scare them off rather than play the hero and get into a fight.

It's best to lock your house securely and fit a burglar alarm. Or go and live in a cave (tip 79).

253

Protect skin from sun

In moderation the sun can give you a healthy colour. Overdo it and you'll suffer from painful sunburn – even sunstroke – and, longer term, there's a danger of skin cancer. Take precautions:

- A sun tan lotion will protect your skin as well as help with the tan, so always apply it.
- If the sun is particularly hot, cover up. Wear light-coloured, loose-fitting clothes.
- Wear a sun hat. This protects the top of your vulnerable head. A good brim will shade your face and neck.

- Sit in the shade when you can. Pick a café table with a parasol – same goes for deckchairs if you can get one.
- Be realistic about your skin. Fair-haired and freckled? You're going to have whitish skin that is sensitive to the sun. Forget your bronze-adonis dreams, you need to cover up in the sun. Wear cool clothes instead.
- Avoid the midday sun whatever your skin type – it's just too powerful and will damage your skin. Especially in a hot country.

254
Make an entrance

- Look your best. What that means in practice depends on the occasion. Jeans and a T-shirt at a black-tie event will get you noticed, but for the wrong reasons. Pay attention to the details like shoes, cuff links and ties. Small things, maybe, but they add up.

- Be confident – but don't confuse confidence with cockiness or arrogance.

- Stand up straight. You'll instantly look three inches taller. Don't overdo it, though, or you'll look like there's a broom up your back. Stay upright but relaxed.

- Smile, but don't force it. If you do, you'll look tense and nervous. Again, the key is to stay relaxed.

- Make eye contact. You'll appear confident and at ease with yourself if you hold someone's gaze rather than looking at your feet.

255
Give an order

- Strike a balance between making your order sound like a request and an instruction. So take a respectful tone while still being clear about what you want to get done.

- You know that something needs to be done, but you may not know the best way of doing it. Empower the person you're giving the order to by letting them use their initiative to find the best way of performing the task. If they succeed, they're more likely to accept an order in the future. A successful order is one where you don't tell someone what to do, you tell them what you want to be done and they do it. Set them the goals, set the boundaries and have the confidence to let them crack on.

- Be explicit. Leave no room for misunderstanding. Give them a time limit that's realistic, rather than just 'now'. In the Army, orders are very clear and are expected to be obeyed without question. The rest of life isn't like that, so build in some flexibility while still getting the job done.

256
Solder a contact

Soldering (melting small amounts of soft metal to create a strong bond) is easy. But so is scalding yourself with hot metal – so work with care.

1 Give the soldering iron time to reach its full temperature while you prepare a tidy, uncluttered work area and make sure that all the elements to be soldered are free of dirt.

2 Begin by 'tinning' your wires and contacts. This involves holding the tip of the iron against each one for a couple of seconds then touching the solder against it just long enough for it to flow on and form a nice shiny coating.

3 Bring together the two elements to be soldered – looping the wire through the contact if applicable. Then hold the iron's tip against the meeting point for about two seconds to heat up both parts. Now touch

the solder against it and, as soon as it melts and flows over the join, move the iron and solder away.

4 You should be left with a smooth, shiny blob – and a connection that will last for decades.

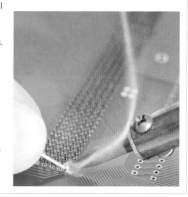

257
Clean a wound

As with any injury or medical emergency, the best advice is to get professional medical help as soon as possible. There may be situations, though, where you have to do what you can. Cleaning a wound is vital in preventing infection.

Use clean water
Clean running water is one of the best things for cleaning a wound. Hold the wound under a running tap.

If you're away from plumbed water you'll have to improvise. If you have a syringe in your kit, squirt clean water forcefully into the wound from 2-4 inches away. Half a litre should wash out most dirt and debris.

If you don't know how clean the water is, add iodine. Shake it up and allow at least five minutes for the iodine to disinfect the water.

You can improvise a syringe using a plastic bag of water with a pinhole in it, or by making a hole in the top of a water bottle.

Remove debris
If no medical help is available, use tweezers sterilised with a lighter flame to carefully pull out foreign bodies. Flush the wound with water to clean out small bits.

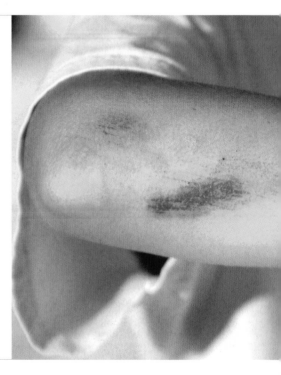

258
Win a fairground prize

Gone are the days of nailed-down coconuts, but the odds are still stacked against you at the fairground. You have to be crafty if you really want that huge Tweetie Pie.

- Stand back and observe other contestants. If you spot a regular winner, watch everything from their stance to their wrist action. Most fairground games can be mastered, so let someone else spend their cash doing so, before nabbing all their techniques.

- Don't be a sucker. If the stall-holder sees you're easily parted from your cash, they'll bleed you dry. Be confident and don't let them know how desperate you are to win. Or how much cash you're willing to spend at their stand.

- Check what prizes are on offer. You may find that winning first time will only net you a small Snoopy. You have to trade up to get the bigger prizes, so only play a game you've mastered. Learn to walk away. Size isn't everything…

259
Skin a rabbit

- Lay the animal on a clean surface (polythene is ideal) on its back with the head towards you.

- Presuming it's already been gutted (tip 219), separate the skin from the meat around the gutting incision.

- Pull enough away to be able to push one hand underneath the skin to grip the rabbit's body tightly.

- It should then be easy to peel off the rest of the skin using your other hand.

- You will find the skin is still attached at the head, legs and tail. These can be removed with scissors or a sharp knife.

- The head is best removed by cutting around the neck, then dislocating the vertebrae with a twist.

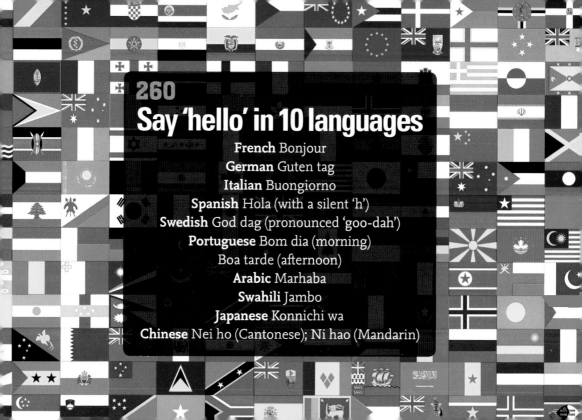

260
Say 'hello' in 10 languages
French Bonjour
German Guten tag
Italian Buongiorno
Spanish Hola (with a silent 'h')
Swedish God dag (pronounced 'goo-dah')
Portuguese Bom dia (morning)
Boa tarde (afternoon)
Arabic Marhaba
Swahili Jambo
Japanese Konnichi wa
Chinese Nei ho (Cantonese); Ni hao (Mandarin)

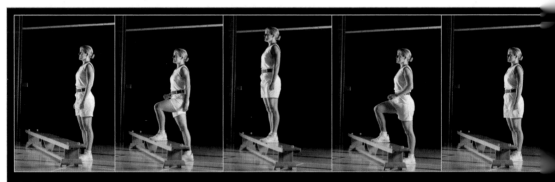

261
Do the perfect step-up

Method:

- Find something sturdy and about 30-40cm off the floor that will comfortably support your body weight (eg a bench).
- Raise one leg to place your foot on the bench.
- Step up onto the bench so both feet are flat on it and you are standing straight.
- Step back down to your original position, leading with the same foot you stepped up with.
- Place your foot on the bench to begin your next step-up.

Tips:

- Alternate the foot you lead with so both legs are trained equally.
- Inhale as you step up and exhale as you step down.
- Concentrate on good technique rather than speed.
- Try to progressively increase the number of step-ups you do in a row each time you exercise as your muscles get stronger.

Muscle groups worked:
Thighs, hamstrings, calves, buttocks

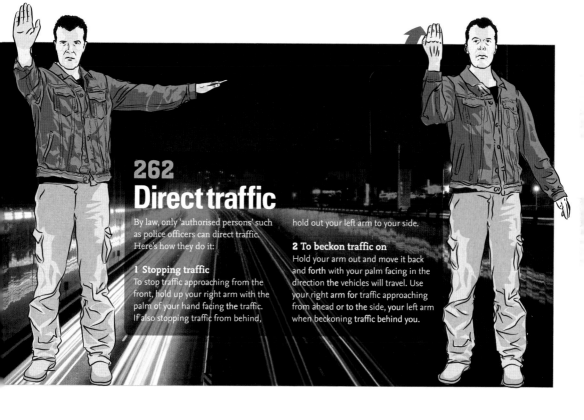

262
Direct traffic

By law, only 'authorised persons' such as police officers can direct traffic. Here's how they do it:

1 Stopping traffic

To stop traffic approaching from the front, hold up your right arm with the palm of your hand facing the traffic. If also stopping traffic from behind,

hold out your left arm to your side.

2 To beckon traffic on

Hold your arm out and move it back and forth with your palm facing in the direction the vehicles will travel. Use your right arm for traffic approaching from ahead or to the side, your left arm when beckoning traffic behind you.

263
Improve your stamina

Slow twitch vs fast twitch

There are two types of muscle fibre, 'fast twitch' and 'slow twitch'. Fast twitch fibres give explosive power. Slow twitch fibres aren't as powerful but can work for longer. It's the slow-twitch fibres you need to train to build stamina. That means less time in the weight room, more time running, swimming or cycling.

Exercise for longer

There's a concept in physical training called 'specificity': if you want to get better at something, practise doing that something.

So if your goal is to run a half-marathon, then running a long way should form the majority of your training.

Build up slowly

You'll need to be dedicated, but nobody can go from couch potato to runner bean overnight. Start off with short sessions of 20-30 minutes with a day off in between. Increase the total length of time spent training, but by no more than 10% each week (or you risk over-training and setting your fitness back). Every month or so take an easy week to give your body time to rest.

Set targets

Have a goal in mind. Make it achievable, but enough of a stretch to motivate you. It should be something you can measure. 'Run a half-marathon in less than two hours' is better than 'run further and faster'.

Training tips for a long run

- Buy the best running shoes you can afford.
- Devise a training programme, write it down in detail and stick with it. Willpower is a winner.
- Control your diet. Dehydration will really hit your performance levels, so fluid intake is crucial.

264
Use binoculars

Yes, you look through one end and things seem much bigger at the other. But there's a little more to it than that.

First, set the diopter – a dial that sets the two sides of your binoculars to match the differences between your eyes.

It's not easy to find targets in a landscape with binoculars, so keep them around your neck until you've identified the precise area you want to look closer at. Then bring the binoculars up to your eyes without moving your head – keep your eyes focused on the target, don't look down at the binoculars.

Grip the binoculars with both hands for maximum stability and adjust the focusing wheel to get a sharp view of your target. Scan the horizon much more slowly than you would with the naked eye.

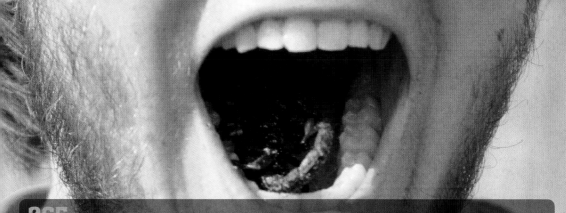

265
Eat bugs

Most insects are edible, but not all of them are nutritious. Some are plain revolting to eat. But if you have to, here's how to munch them.

1 Identify the bug
Never eat a bug you can't identify or that you suspect may be poisonous, and ensure you collect them from an area free of pesticides and contamination.

2 Kill and eat
It's best to avoid eating live bugs, especially those that could bite back. However, don't eat a bug that you find dead. You won't know what it died of and it could be rotten and make you ill.

3 Cook it
Cooking is advised before eating, so either roast your catch swiftly over a fire or fry the critters up in a pan.

4 Hide the taste
If you can't handle eating a bug on its own, use it as a protein supplement for soups and stews. It's easier to eat when you can't recognise it!

5 Remove stings
Bees, wasps and ants are great sources of nutrition but you will have to prepare them. Boiling is the best method. It dissolves the stings of bees and wasps and the formic acid in ants.

Poach an egg

Poaching is reckoned to be one of the hardest ways to cook an egg. Here's how to crack it:

1 Prepare the water
Put a good-sized frying pan on a gentle heat and add 2.5cm of boiling water. Keep the water at a bare simmer throughout cooking.

2 Add the eggs
Use fresh eggs. Break each egg into a cup, then carefully slip them into the water and let them simmer, without covering, for exactly one minute – use a timer.

3 Let them sit
Take the pan off the heat and let the eggs sit in the hot water. Leaving for 10 minutes produces a perfectly set white and soft, creamy yolk.

4 Serve and eat
Lift each egg out of the water with a draining spoon, resting it on a ball of kitchen paper to absorb the water. Serve and eat immediately.

Tip – if you stir the water vigorously before dropping the egg in, the vortex you create will hold the egg together.

Step 1

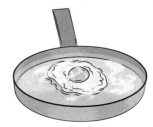

Step 2

Step 3

Step 4

267
Pull off karaoke

Even those who hate it will one day be dragged onto a karaoke stage. Plan for that day and you can face the music without fear.

1 Know your voice
Be honest about how good a singer you are. Can you hold a tune, hit a high note? Sing along to the radio in private and assess yourself.

2 Choose your song
You know your voice, now choose a song to match it. If you're lucky enough to be a good singer you can pick something show-offy. Those less blessed should settle on a simple melody. Note: it must be a popular karaoke song or your planning will be wasted.

3 Know your song
Now get familiar with your song: when the vocals come in, how many choruses there are, the (correct!) lyrics, etc. Practise a lot so on the big night you don't need to even glance at the screen.

4 Perform
Stride up to the stage and greet the crowd. Launch into your song like you are the god of rock incarnate. Engage with the audience, exude confidence and belt it out. Then thank your fans and swagger off stage.

268

Get the last bit of toothpaste out of the tube

If you've forgotten to pick up toothpaste at the shops, there's always a few blobs left in what appears to be an empty tube. Take a pencil (or even your toothbrush), place it on the bottom of the tube and start rolling the tube over it. Keep doing this so the tube wraps around the pencil, and you'll squeeze out the majority of paste left inside. Also, jamming the pencil up into the tube top from below will force paste out of far-flung corners.

Once you think you've got out every last drop, take a pair of scissors, chop the tube in two and wipe your toothbrush on the insides. There'll be enough for at least one more brush.

Beat a stitch

A stitch – that ache you sometimes get in the abdomen while you are running – is caused by a muscle spasm of the diaphragm.

Apply pressure to the pain
The best cure is to slow down or stop. If you need to keep running, press on the pain and release the pressure when you breathe out. Do this several times.

Synchronise your breathing
You can time your breathing so your diaphragm moves down at the same time as your intestines – this decreases stress. If the stitch is on your right side breathe out when your left foot touches the ground, and vice versa. Keep this rhythm going.

Prevent one in the first place
- Warm up before running.
- Keep your upper body warm.
- Don't run soon after eating.
- If it's really cold, breathe through a neck warmer.
- Strengthen your abdominal muscles with exercises.
- Take deep breaths and synchronise your breathing.

270
Ride a horse

The Household Cavalry is one of the most prestigious regiments in the British Army. All its soldiers are taught how to look after and ride a horse. In time they will become experts, but even they must begin with the basics.

1 Mount your horse from the left side, with your left foot in the stirrup and your left hand on the reins.

2 Swing your right leg over and you're on.

3 Get both feet firmly in the stirrups and your hands on the reins. Squeeze your ankles gently into the horse's sides.

4 Keep your back straight and your head up as the horse begins to walk forward.

5 To steer, gently pull the reins left or right and move the opposite leg back slightly.

6 Squeeze harder with your ankles while your horse is already walking, and it will begin to trot. This is a bumpier way to travel, so it helps to move your body in time with the horse's movements, so you're bouncing along in the saddle to the horse's beat.

7 To go from trot to walk or walk to stop, push your heels down, stiffen your lower back, squeeze the horse with your legs and pull the reins towards you.

8 As soon as the horse stops, relax the reins and give it a well deserved pat on the neck.

Cantering and galloping require more skill and practice and are not for beginners. Remember: walk before you trot, before you canter, before you gallop!

This book was brought to you by...

Household Cavalry and Royal Armoured Corps
The Household Cavalry are fine horsemen who take part in the famous Trooping The Colour ceremony. In battle they join the RAC in tanks and recce vehicles.

Royal Artillery
The Royal Regiment of Artillery is the largest – and loudest! – single regiment in the Army. Its soldiers need to be fit enough to lug heavy shells and smart enough to fire them with pinpoint accuracy.

Royal Engineers
The RE builds and maintains structures for the Army, as well as civilian areas affected by disaster or war. All kinds of crafts come under the RE badge, from bricklayers to plumbers.

Royal Signals
The people with the technical know-how, from electricians to IT experts. It's the job of the Royal Signals to set up and maintain reliable and secure communication networks.

Army Air Corps
This is the airborne part of the Army, with its fleet of Apache and Lynx helicopters that can deploy anywhere in the world. It has people working in the air and on the ground in lots of situations, so the Corps has many strengths.

Royal Army Chaplains' Department
The RAChD has 150 chaplains, who provide support, guidance and wisdom to soldiers and their families wherever they are posted. Chaplains are known in the Army as 'padres'.

Royal Logistic Corps
The Army needs a constant stream of equipment, ammunition, fuel, food and clothing. Whatever is required, the RLC's resourceful band of chefs, suppliers, drivers and despatchers can get it delivered.

Royal Army Dental Corps
The RADC is dedicated to ensuring the Army's personnel always have healthy teeth, whether that means preventing problems occurring or treating them when they do. Its staff work in dental centres as well as in the field.

Royal Electrical and Mechanical Engineers

REME is responsible for ensuring all the Army's equipment works – mechanical or electrical, small or large. Roles include metalsmith and vehicle mechanic.

Adjutant General's Corps

A diverse Corps with specialities ranging from admin, HR and finance to management, education, policing and law. The AGC contains lawyers, clerks, bodyguards, teachers and more.

Royal Army Veterinary Corps

The Army's animals are looked after just as well as its people – the RAVC's specialists, from vets to dog trainers, make sure of that.

Infantry

The Infantry forms the largest part of the Army. Infantry soldiers are tough and versatile, with excellent survival and fieldcraft skills. They rely on their initiative to solve problems.

Intelligence Corps

One of the most specialised parts of the British Army, the Intelligence Corps has a wealth of special talents at its disposal. It uses analysts, linguists and all kinds of other clever people to stay one step ahead – at least.

Queen Alexandra's Royal Army Nursing Corps

QARANC has been in existence for over a century, and today provides all parts of the Army Medical Services with highly trained nursing staff dedicated to caring for Army personnel.

Corps of Army Music

The newest Corps in the Army (formed in 1994) is not quite as loud as the Royal Artillery, but much more tuneful! It's bursting with talent and provides the Army's military bands with musicians.

Army Physical Training Corps

The APTC is a specialist Corps with a vital mission: to get all soldiers fit and keep them that way. This Corps has expertise in exercise of all kinds, as well as nutrition and sports science.

INDEX

Cooking & Food

DIY Repairs

Dress sense

Driving

INDEX

INDEX

Survival

And all the rest...

ACKNOWLEDGEMENTS

Editorial team
Editor Ben Ashby
Associate Editor Johnny Aldred
Art Director Adrian Broadway/Ouno
Associate Art Director Paul Yelland

Contributors:
Rick Morris
Matthew Bingham
Richard Purvis
Nat Saunders
Andrew Emery
Chris Hayward
James Hundleby
Simon Guirao
David Burton
David Motton
Johnny Sharp
Sarah Bishop
Adèle Donaghie

Rizwan Mirza
Gwen Campbell
Mark Ranaldi
Sharon Martins

Thanks to:
Ashley Durban
Neil Bradford
Tim Andrews
Robert Kirby
Simon Kanter
Martin Tullett
Andrew Taplin
Brigadier Andrew Jackson
Debrett's

Picture research:
Dominique Campbell

Picture credits
Crown Copyright:
06 RAF
11, 101, 238 Pete Gardner
13 Simon Roberts
18 Gary Tyson, www.defenceimages.mod.uk
25, 28, 38, 46, 56, 57, 70, 92, 97, 115, 118, 123, 153, 160, 164, 187, 211, 240, 246, 261 Duncan Kendall
36 Pete Gardner
45 Andy Earl
53 Sergeant Mike Harvey, www.defenceimages.mod.uk
104, 144, 221, 255 Ted humble Smith
108 Andy Earl
124 Royal Signal Mercury Challenge
143, 203, 270 Richie Hopson
157 Sgt Teresa Pickin, www.defenceimages.mod.uk
197 Harriet Logan
264 Mike Weston, www.defenceimages.mod.uk

Rex Features:
23, 239 Rex Features
63 Nils Jorgensen
77, 149 Everett Collection

For more Army health and fitness tips go to **www.armyfit.mod.uk**